When You Don't Know What to Pray

When You Don't Know
What to
Pray

How to Talk to God about Anything

Linda Evans Shepherd

Revell

a division of Baker Publishing Group
Grand Rapids, Michigan

Published by Revell
a division of Baker Publishing Group
P.O. Box 6287, Grand Rapids, MI 49516-6287

Printed in the United States of America

ISBN-13: 978-1-61664-249-5

For my son, Jim

You are an answer to prayer.
God has great purposes and plans for your life.

Contents

Acknowledgments

This is a book that reflects my own prayer journey. So first, I want to thank the Lord for the circumstances he allowed into my life. It was these circumstances that brought me to my knees, teaching me the deeper secrets of prayer. I also want to thank my precious family; my friend Karen O'Connor, who shared her words of wisdom; my agent, Janet Kobobel Grant; my editor, Vicki Crumpton; and my publisher, Revell. I also thank all the others who helped make this book possible. The stories in this book represent real-life situations. To protect their privacy, many of the names have been changed.

And now I once again say to God, "It's your turn."

Introduction

Beyond the Prayer of Jabez

> Prayer does not mean asking God for all kinds of things we want; it is rather the desire for God himself, the only Giver of Life.
>
> —Sadhu Sundar Singh

I've gotten the same email thousands of times: "God doesn't love me. I know because he hasn't answered my prayers."

Those who write are brave enough to expose the secret thousands more are trying to hide: "God hurt my feelings."

Have you ever been there? Perhaps you're past praying the famous "Jabez prayer" for abundant blessing. Blessings are nice, but when your very survival is at stake and heaven is silent, you may find yourself praying the prayer of King David: "Will you forget me forever?" (Ps. 13:1).

And no wonder. Have you noticed that people today have been hit by more of life's hurricanes than ever before? It seems so many are dealing with a multitude of issues and dilemmas including overwhelming depression, fear, worry, anger, betrayal, broken marriages, health crises, financial emergencies, lost jobs, wayward children or grandchildren, broken lives, natural disasters, bad choices, loss of a loved one, and deeply tragic circumstances.

Could it be that you are dealing with such issues yourself?

Like the little granny on that long-ago Wendy's hamburger commercial who lifted the bun of her skimpy (off-brand) burger to demand, "Where's the beef?" you may be ready to take the lid off your life and demand, "God, if you really love me, then where's the answered prayer, where's the blessing, where's the miracle?"

> To be honest, God did not answer my prayers the way I'd demanded. He did something better. He turned my life into a miracle, and he's ready to do the same thing for you through the pages of this prayer experience.

I understand. But what would happen if you could pray in such a way to erase your doubts and confusion?

You can. This book will help you discover the answers to these questions as you become your own prayer project.

I've seen the power of God transform literally thousands of lives as I teach people how to pray. I, myself, have learned the secrets of prayer through seasons of terrible circumstances. I've learned to push past what felt like unanswered prayer to touch the heart of God. My story is not the usual pie-in-the-sky account. To be honest, God did not answer my prayers the way I'd demanded. He did something better. He turned my life into a miracle, and he's ready to do the same thing for you through the pages of this prayer experience.

But here's the good news. As we pray together, you'll discover:

- God knows where you are.
- He hasn't forgotten you.
- He wants you to know how much he loves you.
- He wants a deeper friendship with you.
- He wants to take you on the journey of a lifetime.

As you might have noticed, this old earth is not heaven, and life can be extremely difficult. So, what would it be worth to know how to reach God, to know he cares? What would it be worth to know that, according to Jeremiah 31:3, "I [God] have loved you with an everlasting love"?

As you'll discover within these pages, it's worth everything.

So don't give up, don't give in to discouragement, and don't grow weary in your prayer life. Take a lesson from Philippians 4:6–7: "Do not be anxious about anything, but in everything, by prayer and petition, with thanksgiving, present your requests to God. And the peace of God, which transcends all understanding, will guard your hearts and your minds in Christ Jesus."

In other words, the first thing you are required to do (as a person of prayer) is to *relax*, then to tell God your needs and your requests with *thanks*.

What would a prayer like that look like? Take a look:

Dear Lord,
I *relax* in you. Here's my problem: _____.
You take it and solve it. And, by the way, *thanks a lot* for this opportunity to bring it to you. I trust you to work this situation out for me.
In Jesus' name,
Amen!

This is so simple, it's easy to miss its profound life-changing power. So let's look deeper. As you pray this prayer, ask your-

11

self, "Did I feel a change?" If not, repeat this simple prayer until you "get" it. What exactly are you trying to get? Only that God wants your permission to handle your problem for you.

Once you "get" it, you'll ask, "Is it really that easy?"

Yes. When you've released your problem to God, you'll start to feel the peace of God transform your heart and mind.

> Like William Temple, a former archbishop of Canterbury, once said, "When I pray, coincidences happen, and when I don't pray, they don't."

If you found this prayer of interest, just wait till you see the other life-transforming prayers you'll pray throughout this book.

As you pray, you'll find answers as you connect with God. But remember, your prayers won't be answered unless they're prayed. Like William Temple, a former archbishop of Canterbury, once said, "When I pray, coincidences happen, and when I don't pray, they don't."[1]

As you grow in your prayer life, you'll begin to see coincidences happen more often than ever.

If you're ready to transform your life, turn the page.

1

Project Prayer

> My prayer today is that we'll feel the loving arms of God
> wrapped around us, and will know in our hearts that he will
> never forsake us as we trust in him.
>
> —Billy Graham

After speaking at an event in Iowa, I was chatting with the
soloist when a grandmother in her early sixties approached us.
Her conference name tag read "Barb" and she said, "Linda, I
appreciated your talk today on joy, but it didn't help me."

Startled, I stared as she continued, "I can't go on. I'm no
good to anyone. It's like I'm already dead."

My friend Jackie's eyebrows shot into her hairline, and she
looked to me as if to say, "Yikes! What do we do?"

I studied the woman before me. Her eyes were dull and
her face hard. She was in incredible emotional pain. "What's
happened to you, Barb?" I asked softly.

Barb frowned, then in one long breath she said, "My husband died last year of a heart attack. I hate my job. I was left
to raise my granddaughters and I'm doing a terrible job. My

son-in-law committed suicide, and I think he had the right idea. I've decided I should kill myself too."

I asked, "Who are you mad at?"

Her blue eyes locked with mine. With a trembling voice she answered, "I loathe myself and I'm mad at God."

> "I loathe myself and I'm mad at God."

I nodded slowly, comprehending her fury, and replied, "That's okay. God's big enough to handle your anger. Do you want to let go of it? Do you want to give God your anger?"

She nodded her head, and together we knelt on the carpet. There on the hotel conference room floor, with conference attendees milling around us and Jackie looking on, Barb let go. She not only gave God her anger, she also gave him her burdens, hurts, and disappointments with a simple prayer, "I give it all to you, Lord, the anger, the burdens, everything."

When we finished, Jackie and I witnessed an amazing transformation. Color returned to Barb's cheeks. Her eyes glistened. The hardness in her face evaporated as if she'd received an instant facelift. It was a stunning moment as we witnessed Barb's return from the dead.

> "I am free. I'm free. I'm free!"

Barb and I stood up and hugged. I said, "Barb, this is what it feels like to be free."

Barb jumped and clapped her hands. "Oh, I didn't know this could happen. I am free. I'm free. I'm free!"

She ran to find her friends to tell them the good news.

Jackie turned to me and grabbed my hand. "What just happened?" she asked.

I smiled. "Barb got set free."

"What did you do to her?"

I shook my head. "I didn't do anything, but God did. He simply answered Barb's prayer when she gave him her anger and her burdens."

"How did you know what to pray?" Jackie asked.

"Unfortunately, I've seen this a lot," I replied.

We turned and stood quietly as we watched a new Barb, a younger, more vibrant Barb, hug her daughter and laugh as she related how God had set her free.

Jackie said, "That's the most amazing thing I've ever seen."

In my work as a speaker to groups across the country, I've often led my audiences in the same kind of prayers and have been incredibly privileged to see dramatic results.

If you've ever experienced a powerful prayer, you know the word *amazing* doesn't begin to describe how awesome it is to touch the heart of God. But, are we really touching God or is he reaching down to touch us? The answer is clear: we have it both ways.

Guaranteed Results?

While I can teach you the whys and the hows of prayer, I cannot guarantee the results because God cannot be put into a box. He cannot be bought or sold or made to perform on demand. God is majestic and mysterious, and his ways are not our ways. A man named Simon found that out in Acts 8:9–24.

Simon was a well-known figure in Samaria. He was a showman—a gifted magician using his charisma and skill to all but convince the locals that he was the Messiah. So when Philip arrived on the scene, performing genuine miracles in the name of the true Messiah—Jesus of Nazareth—Simon believed and was baptized.

He followed Philip around town in amazement because Philip did not perform sleight-of-hand magic but real wonders that not only impressed the crowds but changed the lives of those he touched. The old blind beggar who regularly sat in the market now had his sight. The cripple everyone had known since her birth could now walk. The demon-possessed man who had lived outside the city gate was now clothed and in his right mind. This was no rabbit in a hat but the power of God, and Simon knew it.

When Peter and John heard about the revival in Samaria, they came down from Jerusalem to join Philip in the work. That's when Simon saw something amazing. He saw Peter pray simple prayers that caused the power of God to fall on believers, enabling them to perform great wonders and miracles. This gave Simon an idea.

Simon had made his living working the crowds with his showmanship until the power of God upstaged him. But if this power could be transferred to him, he saw a marketable fit, perfect for his business plan. Simon reasoned that if Peter would simply lay hands on him to bestow the power of God, then he could be back on the platform. He could once more stand before adoring crowds, healing the sick while hawking God. What could be better?

Simon decided to approach Peter, perhaps by inviting Peter and his friends into his home to share an evening meal. He probably waited till their stomachs were full and then ever so casually put the idea before them.

I imagine the conversation went something like this: "Peter, the work you do is phenomenal. I am so amazed by the power of God, the anointing, and how it changes lives. I would love to do what you do. And I'd be willing to pay for the privilege. Name your price and we can start our own 'God franchise.' I know people would pay for these incredible healings. We could help God answer the prayers of the masses. We could be rich and famous. Think about it, Peter. I've got my checkbook out, my pen is ready. All you have to do is name your price."

It's at this moment I can imagine the sound of a needle scraping across a vinyl record. *Errrrkkkkkkk!*

Peter looked up in shock. The anointing of God as a business proposition? The nerve!

> The anointing of God as a business proposition? The nerve!

Can you imagine Peter's reply? Well, you don't have to, because it's recorded in verses 20–24.

Peter answered:

> May your money perish with you, because you thought you could buy the gift of God with money! You have no part or share in this ministry, because your heart is not right before God. Repent of this wickedness and pray to the Lord. Perhaps he will forgive you for having such a thought in your heart. For I see that you are full of bitterness and captive to sin.

Then Simon answered, "Pray to the Lord for me so that nothing you have said may happen to me."

Poor Simon, I don't think he understood what he'd asked for. He'd asked to harness the power of God—for profit. To harness God! Ay-yi-yi!

Does the church ever do this? Try to harness God or his power?

Ahem. Well, yes. Have you ever heard a TV evangelist say, "Put your money in the envelope and send it to me as your seed of faith, *then the miracle you long for will be yours*"?

Errrrkkkkkkk!

I know most of these men and women mean well. Many have ministries worth keeping on the air. But we must remember Simon's lesson: you simply cannot buy or force the anointing of God. You cannot sell it, promise it, put it in an envelope, or send it in the mail. Why? God is God! God is awesome, majestic, and most of all, he does not wear a harness or come with a steering wheel.

> God is God! God is awesome, majestic, and most of all, he does not wear a harness or come with a steering wheel.

You can't force him to do your bidding. You can't make promises to God with strings attached, you can't trade favors with God, and you can't bribe God with a payoff. Don't even think about it.

I know what I'm saying. I had to learn this lesson the hard way. Let me share how I not only got this concept through my thick head but also finally figured out how to pray a powerful prayer that saved my life.

The Prayer That Changed Me

Twenty years ago my baby was thrown into the freeway in a violent car accident. She was rushed to the ER by a speeding ambulance as I sobbed out prayers on her behalf. At first the doctors thought she'd be okay and put her on a respirator to "assist" her breathing. But during the night her brain began to swell, and by morning she'd slipped into a coma.

But I knew "coma" was not a problem God couldn't solve, so I prayed the prayer of faith, practically demanding God bring Laura back to me.

In the weeks, then months that followed, I clung to my faith that God would answer my prayer. Almost four months later, when the hospital staff had finished their evaluation of Laura, they called a meeting to share their findings.

I could hardly wait. They were about to give me the plan of how they were going to pull my daughter out of the coma. But instead, twenty-one healthcare professionals pronounced their verdicts.

"Your daughter is not in a coma. She's in a vegetative state."

"She'll never wake up."

"Sorry. There's no hope."

"No hope."

No hope.

I sat stoic, holding back the tears that would have stopped the meeting. I may have been a brave actress, but I felt numb, violated, and shocked.

Later that night I sat in the stillness of my daughter's hospital room, holding her hand, watching for signs of life. As I studied her, I leaned over and kissed her cherubic face. "Honey, it's Mommy. I love you . . . I know you're in there. I'm waiting . . ."

The words caught in my throat. The mechanical breathing of her respirator jarred my thoughts. A strange mood of uncertainty settled over me. I looked at the child I'd prayed so hard to keep. *She's really in there, isn't she?*

I stood up, flipped off the light, and shut her door.

What if the doctors are right and Laura never wakes up? I thought as I spread a blanket in the window seat across from Laura's bed.

A new thought punctured my tired spirit. *Just who am I trying to fool? I need to face facts. Laura will never awaken. She'll live the rest of her life as a vegetable, hooked to life support.*

I tried to stifle the emotions that threatened to boil over as Laura's respirator mocked, *No hope, no hope, no hope.* My chest constricted as I gasped for air. Everything seemed so different, so pointless. Laura, I decided, would be better off if she were . . . to die. After all, I concluded, I couldn't allow her to live in this suspended state of life, could I?

A plan rose from my grief.

I could turn off the alarms and unplug the vent from the wall. It would be so simple, except . . . except, I wondered, *If I kill my daughter, how could I live with myself? How could I face my husband or my parents?*

The moonlight reflected on my bottle of painkillers. If I swallowed them . . . no one would find us until morning. Laura and I could escape this living hell together.

Just as my plan seemed like the best solution, I found my hand resting on my belly. My hidden child was only two weeks old, but I knew he was there.

My thoughts slowly cleared. *How can I kill myself? How can I kill Laura? A new life is growing inside of me, the life of a person who has the right to live!*

My reason returned, and I prayed a powerful prayer: "Lord, I'm willing to wait—despite the pain and the cost. I'm willing to wait and trust in you, no matter what."

> Lord, I'm willing to wait—despite the pain and the cost. I'm willing to wait and trust in you, no matter what.

That night I cried myself to sleep, terrified of the future and terrified of the murders I'd almost committed.

Despite that night of terror followed by my surrender to God, Laura remained unchanged. Over the following months, the hospital sent her home, where she continued to sleep as my girth grew. Almost nine months later, as I nestled her newborn brother into her arms for the first time, her eyes opened to awareness. As Laura held her baby brother, God woke her from her coma! He'd answered my prayer of trust, which as it turns out is the "real" prayer of faith.

Prayer Offers Reconciliation with God

You might be thinking this prayer stuff isn't what you thought it would be. You're right. It's even better.

Better?

Yes, but there are a few concepts you must understand. First, you must realize that God loves us with an everlasting love. We were created in his image—a great distinction from the other creatures on this planet—so we could be in friendship with him.

However, friendship with God can seem impossible when we feel angry at:

- God
- ourselves
- others

It's also difficult to achieve friendship with God when we feel he is angry with us. Powerful prayer can offer reconciliation. Dictionary.com defines *reconcile* as follows:

To reestablish a close relationship

To settle or resolve

To bring (oneself) to accept

To make compatible or consistent

If we were to take this definition and apply it to our relationship with God, we would say to reconcile with God means:

- To reestablish a close relationship between *God and humanity*
- To settle or resolve *a difficulty with God*

- To bring (oneself) to accept that *you can trust God with your circumstances*
- To make compatible or consistent that *you can know God as a friend*

Effective prayer is not prayer that bosses God. It's something completely different. Effective prayer is prayer that trusts God no matter what.

Unanswered Prayer

We label prayers that seem to go unanswered or ignored as rejection from God.

I hear it again and again in my GodTest.com email, "God did not answer my prayer the way I asked. Therefore, he does not love me and I have nothing to live for. I'm planning to kill myself, for God has forgotten me.—Signed, Why Not Be Dead"[1]

Errrrkkkkkkk!

I write back:

Dear "Why Not,"

I'm sorry to hear of your difficulties. Sometimes it seems life isn't fair. But that doesn't mean God has forgotten you. God loves you and has a plan for your life.

Before you think of ending your life, consider what you are saying to God when you make a decision for suicide. You're saying, "God, I can't trust you. I'll have to take care of this matter myself and end my life. I am not willing to go through this season of pain to reach your plan."

Be assured God has heard your cries and he weeps with you. Did you know that when Jesus lived on this earth, he had a good friend named Lazarus who died while he was out of town? When Jesus returned to Bethany, he wept with

Lazarus's sisters because it pained him to see his friends experience such great grief. It pained him to see such suffering even though joy was only moments away. Jesus wept even though he was about to resurrect Lazarus from the dead.

Just as Jesus loved Lazarus's grieving family, he loves you with a tender, everlasting love. He wants you to understand that your pain grieves him. (See 2 Cor. 1:4.)

He wants you to cast your burdens and pain on him. (See Ps. 55:22.) He wants you to give him all the circumstances that have hurt you. (See 1 Peter 5:7.) When you really let go, he is able to shoulder much of the pain you are carrying.

Someday, your circumstances may change. But even if they remain difficult, you will experience joy again. Regardless, when you learn to pray the prayer of trust, God will resurrect the problems of your life into a miracle.

Pray this prayer:

Lord, I give you my circumstances—all of them. Please carry them for me. Through an act of my will, I have decided to live. I understand that if I am to trust you, I must push through my pain. Thank you that this dark night will not last forever. Thank you that you hear me and that you have not forgotten me. Thank you that I can trust you with my very life. I choose to do that right now.

In the name of Jesus,
Amen.

Stay in the struggle, stay in the race, but dedicate it all to God.

From one who cares,
Linda

P.S. Your life will not change overnight, but as you trust God—one minute, one hour, one day at a time—you will soon discover that he has led you out of this dark place and has provided you with hope and a future.

> Your life will not change overnight, but as you trust God—one minute, one hour, one day at a time—you will soon discover that he has led you out of this dark place and has provided you with hope and a future.

Casting Off Anxieties

Regardless of whether or not we have been in a place of despair like "Why Not," we can all learn this lesson: when we try to carry our burdens and worries by ourselves, they become the very things that separate us from God.

As it says in 1 Peter 5:7 (RSV), "Cast all your anxieties on him, for he cares about you." We will revisit this verse in future chapters, but for now, turn it into a prayer:

> Dear Father,
> I give you my worries and cares. Please carry them for me and draw me into a more intimate relationship with you.
> In Jesus' name,
> Amen.

Our prayer project is just beginning. Wait until you see where it takes us next.

2

The Five Keys to Power Prayer

Any concern too small to be turned into a prayer is too small to be made into a burden.

—Corrie ten Boom

I've often wondered, *Why pray? I mean, does God really "need" our prayers?*

Yes! I believe God is waiting for us, his church, to call out to him in prayer, agreeing with his purposes. We know we cannot accomplish his purposes without him, but I believe he is waiting for our prayers of agreement as well as our obedience before he will move to accomplish his purposes through us. One thing is clear, God moves when we pray.

If our prayer work is so important to the purposes of God, we need to understand these five prayer keys:

- Come to God humbly
- Repent
- Ask

- Submit
- Praise

Let's explore these areas in detail.

Come to God Humbly

First, it is an awesome privilege that we can come to God. Jesus Christ himself extended the invitation in Matthew 11:28: "Come to me, all you who are weary and burdened, and I will give you rest."

Notice Jesus didn't say, "Hey, when you get your act together, when you are perfect or deserving, then you can come to me."

Instead, he calls us to approach him in the middle of our struggles, in the middle of our everyday lives.

That's good news. So is the fact that we can come to God as sons and daughters. Second Corinthians 6:18 says, "'I will be a Father to you, and you will be my sons and daughters,' says the Lord Almighty."

A loving God as our father? That's pretty heady.

When my son Jim was a teenager, I loved to see him come to me with his problems. I didn't always try to fix them because there were some battles he needed to struggle through to become a better man. But his willingness to share his world with me drew us closer.

When Jim was sixteen, he got his first job. He was hired to wear a sign and wave at cars outside a local business. But one day when I drove him to pick up his first paycheck, he came back to the car empty-handed. "They wouldn't pay me," he said.

As this business had already given me reason to be concerned, I was not surprised. So when Jim asked me to go inside and talk to the owner for him, I agreed.

Now, if Jim had tried to drag me into a meeting with this business owner, come to the car yelling about what he deserved, or insisted that I tell this man off, I don't think I would have gone inside. But Jim approached me humbly. When he did, my "mother's instinct" kicked in. I got out of the car and requested to see the owner.

When I sat down across from this man who had treated my son unfairly, I have to admit my heart hammered in my chest. But I kept my cool. "All I'm asking," I told him, "is that you treat my son fairly. If you don't, my son won't return for his next shift."

That's when the owner pulled out his checkbook to correct the "mistake."

> Sometimes he'll let us struggle as a means to help us become better people or to accomplish a greater purpose.

We are sons and daughters of God. He loves us. When we have a problem, we can go to him and humbly ask him to move on our behalf. We know he hears us as it says in 1 John 5:14–15: "This is the confidence we have in approaching God: that if we ask anything according to his will, he hears us. And if we know that he hears us—whatever we ask—we know that we have what we asked of him."

Sometimes he'll let us struggle as a means to help us become better people or to accomplish a greater purpose.

Yet he often intervenes directly into the situation.

I believe our attitude plays a big part in the process. I believe that was the case in Luke 18:10–14 when Jesus told this parable:

> Two men went up to the temple to pray, one a Pharisee and the other a tax collector. The Pharisee stood up and prayed about himself: "God, I thank you that I am not like other men—robbers, evildoers, adulterers—or even like this tax collector. I fast twice a week and give a tenth of all I get."

But the tax collector stood at a distance. He would not even look up to heaven, but beat his breast and said, "God, have mercy on me, a sinner."

I tell you that this man, rather than the other, went home justified before God. For everyone who exalts himself will be humbled, and he who humbles himself will be exalted.

How clear can it be? We need to come to God humbly. We are not his master, he is our master.

Repent

Repent is the dirty little word much avoided in the church. We don't mind letting folks know that God will forgive their sins through Jesus, but we don't want to "scare them off" with the concept of repentance. *Repent*, according to Dictionary.com, means "to make a change for the better as a result of remorse or contrition for one's sins."

> We need to come to God humbly. We are not his master, he is our master.

God forbid one would have to change for the better. That might not be fun or even politically correct. Right?

A schoolteacher discovered a six-year-old student chewing on a lead bullet. The student was having fun until the teacher took the bullet away.

"What if it had blown up in his mouth?" she later asked me.

"That couldn't have happened," I said. "Lead poisoning would be my chief concern."

"I hadn't even thought of that," the teacher said.

In many ways sin is just like lead poisoning. How many of us would let our babies suckle lead? No way! We love our kids and we'd make them stop.

It's the same with God. He sees the hidden danger and advises us to repent (or stop) because he cares—because he loves us. When we turn from our sins, two things happen:

- We stop hurting ourselves and/or others.
- We develop a closer relationship with God.

It turns out sin separates us from God. God will forgive us through the sacrifice of Jesus, but that doesn't mean it's wise to play with a loaded gun. Sin not only poisons; it kills.

If you found your six-year-old chewing on a lead bullet or discovered your teenage daughter playing a game of Russian roulette, you'd tell them to stop. You'd ask them to surrender the lead bullet for their own good.

It's the same with God. He's not a killjoy. He simply wants to protect us.

> If you want to remove all barricades in your relationship with God, take Jesus' advice and repent. Then the kingdom of heaven will be closer than ever.

Did you know that the first message Jesus preached had to do with repenting? You can read it in Matthew 4:17: "From that time on Jesus began to preach, 'Repent, for the kingdom of heaven is near.'"

If you want to remove all barricades in your relationship with God, take Jesus' advice and repent. Then the kingdom of heaven will be closer than ever.

My plumber told me he'd been called to do a job in a crawl space beneath a home in the Colorado foothills. When he opened the door to crawl inside, the entire space vibrated with the sound of rattlers. He turned to the homeowner and said, "I'll come back when you get rid of your little pets."

That leads me to ask, do you have pet sins?

When we entertain such "charmers," it is hard for us to make room for God. In the following pages, I'll give you tips on how to free yourself from such dangerous creatures of habit. It turns out that "pet" sins don't just keep you company, they take you prisoner. It's time to be set free.

My plumber's story reminds me of a nest of baby rattlesnakes I once met while hiking in the mountains above Durango, Colorado. Here I was, minding my own business, when I came to a lovely clearing that overlooked the valley below. There, in a patch of sunlight, glowed a tiny pond. But what captured my attention was the fallen log that would make the perfect rest stop.

As I approached the log, something wiggly caught my eye. I looked down to see I was standing in the middle of a nest of baby rattlesnakes.

Now this was not a choice I'd purposefully made. I just happened to be in the wrong place at the wrong time.

Did you know that the bite of a baby rattlesnake, not to mention a nest full of baby rattlesnakes, can be lethal? I knew it.

I began to scream and dance on those slithering creatures beneath my thick leather hiking boots. I remember looking to my husband for help, but he was useless because he couldn't stop laughing.

Suddenly I saw myself from his perspective. (Did I mention I had on my thick leather hiking boots?)

You see, there was no way those little snakes could bite me unless I got so hysterical I fell on top of them. My dancing was what put me in danger. The solution? I stepped toward my chuckling husband.

"Why didn't you help me?" I demanded.

"You didn't need me," he said. "You had the power to save yourself and you did."

Could it be that you are standing in a nest of fanged danger? (No, I'm not talking about your family, unless you are in danger from violence.) I'm talking about sin. You may have stepped right into the middle of it, perhaps through no fault of your own. Regardless of how you got there, there is a solution. Just step away. Turn around. Back off.

Yes, you can do that. Your path of escape might start with the following prayer:

Dear Lord,

I'm standing right smack in the middle of sin. And I'm sorry, really sorry. For whatever reason, I seem to be stuck. So, could you give me your power to break free? I choose, by an act of my will, to stop—to turn from my sin. Lord, give me your power to do so.

I bind the power of the evil one and say to him, you have no power or authority over me. I have been bought with a price—the power of the blood and resurrection of Jesus. I claim his righteousness, not mine. So back off. Hands off. I don't belong to you, and I break the power you've had over me in this situation.

Thank you, Father, for setting me free in the name of Jesus Christ, your Son. Amen.

Wow! That's a prayer to repeat whenever you find yourself mired in a sinful situation or attitude.

Ask

Yes, you have the right to ask anything—big or small—of God.

I was once in a church service when the pastor asked that we turn and pray for our neighbor. That's how I met Kate.

She asked me to pray for her aching back. "It's been killing me for years," she told me.

So when it was time to pray, I prayed this simple prayer: "Lord, please heal Kate's back, in the name of Jesus."

I didn't see a lightning bolt and neither did Kate. After the service, Kate and I exchanged business cards. Though I didn't see Kate again, I received a Christmas card from her. It said, "You probably don't remember me, but one day you prayed that God would heal my back. He did. It's been six months, and I no longer have pain."

> Our job is simply to ask. He's the one who answers.

I couldn't stop staring at Kate's handwritten words. God had really healed her after my simple prayer? Why? Because it fit his good purpose. How had he healed her? Through his power—for God is the power behind prayer. It was not my power. Our job is simply to ask. He's the one who answers.

When he answers the details of our simplest prayers, we feel his love.

A couple of weeks ago I needed a straight pin to pin a note to a tiny rag doll's dress before popping it into the mail the next day. I searched high and low, but there were no straight pins in my entire house. So I prayed a simple prayer. "Lord, tonight would you please have someone bring me a straight pin?"

Then I realized how silly it was to ask the King of the universe for a straight pin, so I said, "Oh, never mind, God. I'll go buy some straight pins tomorrow. Please forgive me for praying such a silly prayer." Then, to be honest, I forgot about my request.

That night the members of my Bible study arrived at my home. We were getting ready to pray when Mona turned to Bobbie. "Hold still," she said. "You've got a straight pin stuck in your sleeve."

I almost jumped out of my chair. God had answered my silly prayer? "Do you want that straight pin?" I asked Bobbie.

"Nope," she said.

"Can I have it? I prayed someone would bring me a straight pin tonight."

"No, you didn't," Bobbie said, laughing.

"Yes, I really did."

We all laughed, and then began to talk about it. Why would God answer such a silly prayer about a straight pin when he must have so many bigger concerns like poverty and world peace? We decided it was an intimate way to let me know that he had heard my prayer and that he loved me, that he loved us all.

If I'd never prayed my silly prayer, I would have missed an opportunity to be touched by the sweetness of God's gesture toward me, toward my entire Bible study.

God may say no to one or more of our prayers. But if we don't ask, we don't give him the opportunity to say yes.

Try this simple prayer:

Dear Lord,

I come to you, because I am your child, and I humbly ask:

_____.

In the name of Jesus,
Amen.

Submit

The apostle Paul was one of the greatest believers who ever lived. It seems from biblical accounts that he had a hotline to God. Great miracles were often bestowed from heaven whenever Paul requested them. However, Paul had what many would call a great prayer failure. He reported in a letter to the Christians in Corinthians (2 Cor. 12:7) that Satan sent him a thorn in his flesh to torment him.

A lot of theologians have wondered what the thorn was. Some think it could have been heartache or temptation, while others believe it was trouble with his eyes, pain, or sickness. Still others think it was betrayal by fellow believers, while some say it was strife caused by his fellow Jews.

Though we don't know the exact nature of the thorn, we do know Paul finally accepted it after asking God to remove it three times. Paul was wise and bowed to God's greater purpose. In Paul's own words in verse 7, he concluded that the thorn served "to keep me from becoming conceited because of these surpassingly great revelations." Paul recognized that though God didn't send the thorn, God used it to make him a better man.

God didn't always do what Paul asked him to do. Paul accepted that. He submitted to God's decision. He didn't complain, he didn't threaten suicide, he didn't pout. Instead, he saw the value of the thorn. He saw that his thorn belonged to a rose of purpose.

> Instead, he saw the value of the thorn. He saw that his thorn belonged to a rose of purpose.

Starting in verse 9 we read Paul's words, "But [God] said to me, 'My grace is sufficient for you, for my power is made perfect in weakness.' Therefore I will boast all the more gladly about my weaknesses, so that Christ's power may rest on me. That is why, for Christ's sake, I delight in weaknesses, in insults, in hardships, in persecutions, in difficulties. For when I am weak, then I am strong."

Though Paul didn't get the answer he wanted, he got something better. He found God's strength in exchange for his own human weakness. And Paul wasn't the only one who prayed such a powerful prayer, demonstrating his trust in the Father. So did Jesus.

In Jesus' final moments before his arrest that led to his crucifixion, he knelt in the Garden of Gethsemane to pray. If it had been me, I would have prayed, "Spare me, oh Lord! Take away this cup and get me out of here!" Jesus, however, prayed, "Father, if you are willing, take this cup from me; yet not my will, but yours be done" (Luke 22:42).

Jesus could have prayed for his own rescue, but instead he bought our salvation with his very blood. Jesus' prayer prevented our suffering rather than his own.

Jesus submitted to God's will through his powerful prayer for the greater purpose—a purpose that not only saved our lives but made it possible for our sins to be forgiven so that we could become friends with God.

The next time you face a difficulty, try the simple prayer of Jesus:

> Dear Father,
> If you are willing, take this cup from me; yet not my will, but yours be done.
> In the name of Jesus,
> Amen.

Praise

The apostle Paul said it very well in Ephesians 5:20: "Always giving thanks to God the Father for everything, in the name of our Lord Jesus Christ."

Oftentimes, it seems that thanking God is the last thing we think of doing. But it's the first thing that should come to mind. For example, not long ago I heard that a friend was holding a grudge against me. Though I dislike conflict, I decided to confront my friend. But before I did so, I first stopped to thank God for both my friend and for what God was doing in our relationship. That prayer of thanksgiving helped me face my friend, not only without anger but also with eager anticipation that God was in control and that he would move on our behalf.

He did! I again rejoiced when the conflict was easily resolved. I still rejoice because my friend and I are better friends for facing the misunderstanding in a spirit of love. How glad I am that I came to God with a spirit of thanksgiving instead of going to my friend in a spirit of anger.

The problem for a lot of us is that when we look at our circumstances we often see them through the eyes of fear instead of the eyes of trust. When we can't immediately see a solution to a problem, we forget God is at work.

> The problem for a lot of us is that when we look at our circumstances we often see them through the eyes of fear instead of the eyes of trust. When we can't immediately see a solution to a problem, we forget God is at work.

The lesson? We should trust God and continually thank him through all our circumstances.

One spring afternoon, dark clouds released a sudden downfall of pea-sized hail that bounced across my yard. I ran to the front door to watch, expecting the dramatic storm to quickly pass. To my horror, the hail grew larger and beat down my walkway tulips. That's when I became disturbed by the noise above my head. *Crack! Pop!* The sound of hail hitting my roof was thunderous. I ran to Laura's room, thinking I would need to comfort a frightened child. But Laura wasn't frightened, she was laughing. From her window, I could see that the hail had grown larger still—now the size of golf balls.

Instead of the horror I'd felt moments earlier, I got caught up in Laura's excitement. I said, "Laura, it looks like God is throwing ice cubes."

We laughed together and talked about the awesome power and strength of God. I kept laughing, that is, until the storm passed. That's when I went outside to view the damage. Split-wooden shingles from my roof were strewn around the yard, and I knew my roof was totaled.

Once again I was horrified. But I needn't have been. A few weeks later we were finally able to replace our old flammable roof with a stronger, nonflammable roof, all paid for by our insurance company. Despite my initial worries, the storm had been a blessing.

As I thought about that storm, I realized my assessment of it depended on my perspective. From a homeowner's perspective, the storm had turned into a blessing. From an insurer's perspective, the storm was surely viewed as a curse. From a roofer's perspective, the storm was a bonanza. And from my daughter's perspective, the storm was a joyful experience and an awesome demonstration of the power of God.

Could it be there are storms in our lives where our perspective may not match God's? Even when it's impossible to see our circumstances from God's point of view, we can still trust him with anything and everything. And because we trust him, we can praise him no matter what. So, praise him even in your darkest hour, because someday, whether on this side of heaven or the other, we will see what God was doing all along.

So why wait? Use your faith and trust to celebrate what God is doing no matter how your circumstances may appear.

Try this thank-you prayer in your next (or current) difficulty:

Dear Lord,
    Thank you for being with me in this storm. Thank you that I can trust you with the results of this storm. Thank you that the results will be for good because I love you and am

called according to your purpose. Thank you that I can call
on you to bind the enemy from this storm.

In Jesus' name,
Amen.

Putting It Together

Now that we've analyzed the elements of a powerful prayer, did
you know that it's exactly how Jesus taught us to pray in the
Lord's Prayer? Check it out in Matthew 6:9–13 (NKJV).

Come to God Humbly
Our Father in heaven,
Hallowed be Your name.

Submit
Your kingdom come.
Your will be done
On earth as it is in heaven.

Ask
Give us this day our daily bread.
And forgive us our debts,
As we forgive our debtors.

Repent
And do not lead us into temptation,
But deliver us from the evil one.

Praise
For Yours is the kingdom and the power and the glory forever. Amen.

Jesus is teaching about prayer in this passage, and this is
meant to be a template for all of our prayer projects. Aldous

Huxley, a British novelist born in the late 1800s, said, "The Lord's Prayer is repeated daily by millions who have not the slightest intention of letting anyone's will be done but their own."[1]

Errrrkkkkkkk!

Ouch, we'd better make sure we don't fall into that category.

Recap

We've looked at the outline Jesus used to teach us to pray. Try composing your own prayer using the following outline:

Come to God humbly:

_____

Submit (to God's will):

_____

Ask (make a request):

_____

Repent:

_____

Praise God:

_____

In Jesus' own personal prayer life he often praised his Father. In Luke 10, we read the account of seventy-two joyful disciples who were sent by Jesus as "workers into his harvest field" (v. 2). At the disciples' good report, Jesus was filled with joy through the Holy Spirit. Instead of keeping his joy to himself, he shared it with his Father by saying, "I praise you, Father, Lord of heaven and earth, because you have hidden these things from the wise and learned, and revealed them to little children. Yes, Father, for this was your good pleasure" (v. 21).

Jesus even praised his Father for hearing his prayer at the moment he was preparing to raise his friend Lazarus from the dead. "So they took away the stone. Then Jesus looked up and said, 'Father, I thank you that you have heard me'" (John 11:41).

I love that prayer. This is a praise we should repeat often, because it was through the sacrifice of Jesus that the Father can hear our prayers as our Father. Thank you, Father. Thank you, Lord Jesus.

When to Pray

And finally, let's take a look at when to pray. We need to pray:

- In important decisions (see Luke 6:12–13)
- In the morning (see Ps. 5:2–3)
- Day and night (see Ps. 88:1)
- Three times a day (see Ps. 55:16–17)
- Without ceasing (see 1 Thess. 5:17)

I like the way Rick Warren puts it in his book *The Purpose Driven Life*.

He [God] wants to be included in *every* activity, every conversation, every problem, and even every thought. You can carry on a continuous, open-ended conversation with him throughout your day, talking with him about whatever you are doing or thinking at that moment. "Praying without ceasing" means conversing with God while shopping, driving, working, or performing any other everyday tasks.[2]

What's Next

In the following chapters, you'll learn how to pray powerfully for yourself and others in the following situations:

- When you can't feel God's presence
- When you're overwhelmed
- When you've been betrayed
- When you've made mistakes
- When everything goes wrong
- When you experience financial difficulties
- When it's hard to trust God
- When you don't understand God's answers
- When you don't know how to respond
- When you lack joy

Turn the pages and discover how these powerful prayers will change your life.

3

What to Pray for Yourself

We must alter our lives in order to alter our hearts, for it is
impossible to live one way and pray another.

—William Law

Get ready for a season of prayer that will change your life.
Lock your door. Take the phone off the hook. Hide in the
closet. Even if you can't get away from the people and dis-
tractions that surround you, you can still be alone with God.
All you have to do is clear a mental space in your head and
heart.

One of my daughter's therapists travels Boulder County
in her van, which she's turned into a mobile speech and language classroom for kids. Pam says that every morning when
she climbs inside, she clears off the passenger seat for Jesus.
She prays, "Lord, could you go with me today as I visit my
students?"

I love that!

Let's invite Jesus to go with us as we pray our way through this chapter.

Dear Jesus,

Could you go with me through this chapter and through this book? Could you open the eyes of my heart to show me everything you have for me? Help me to focus on you, your Word, and all you have to teach me.

Amen.

Yes! You've just asked Jesus to read this chapter and this book with you and to you. This is cooler than a refreshing summer rain.

God's Love for You

Before we get into the actual act of self-prayer, I would like to take this moment for a commercial break from my sponsor. The Lord of the universe has a special message for you. Okay, I know you've heard it before, but it's time you believed it with your entire being.

The message is this: GOD LOVES YOU!

Yeah, yeah, you know that. But do you really get it all the way down to your toenails? Let me say it one more time: GOD LOVES YOU! Now, say it aloud: GOD LOVES ME!

Really! Truly!

Until this concept captures your heart, you will find it difficult to pray for yourself, because of all people, you alone know how undeserving of God's love you are.

It's true that on occasion you've been known to sin, lie, cheat, gossip . . . well, I don't need to list all your faults. I'm assuming you already know most of them as I know mine. However, as I've discovered, knowing you aren't perfect makes you question your worth. Based on what you know about you and what I know about me, neither of us deserves God's love. Yet he loves us anyway.

Look at it this way: God's love for us is supernatural. Despite our shortcomings, God cares about the details of our lives. My life. Your life. *Really.*

Here's yet another barrier to prayer; it's hard to pray for yourself when you doubt God. You may wonder, *How can there be a loving God when we see this broken world full of tragedy and suffering?*

The message is this: GOD LOVES YOU!

I call that the Divine Question, which of course has a divine answer. Let me tell you a story.

At a point before time, a terrible battle raged between God and our mortal enemy, Satan, in the heavenlies. Satan (Lucifer) led a revolt against God, and he and his minions were cast out of heaven, like a falling star.

Then one day, after time began, Lucifer tricked Adam and Eve out of their innocence in the Garden of Eden. There, Eve fell for his line about eating the forbidden fruit: "You will be *like* God, 'knowing good and evil'" (Gen. 3:5, emphasis mine).

Well, yes, this was all true to a point. But when Eve bit into the fruit and swallowed Satan's lie, this first sin opened her eyes so that she *could* see good and evil. She could see that her disobedience (along with Adam's) had poisoned their very souls with evil. The fallout? Adam and Eve lost the intimacy they had shared with God because their sin separated them from God's holiness. They were cast out of his beautiful garden to scratch out their living in the thorns of sin. But worst of all, there were no more walks and talks with God in the cool of the evening, as they were exiled from the lover of their souls. Was there no hope, no cure for this poison that separated them from God, their beloved?

You would think this great rift between God and humanity would cause God to give up on people altogether and wipe our species off the face of the earth. But despite this rift caused by sin, he continued to love the people he had created. He closely followed their trials and tribulations and heard them when they cried out to him.

Once, when his people, the Israelites, were in slavery in Egypt, God sent Moses to win their release from the pharaoh. After experiencing God's wrath, Pharaoh finally set the people free, and Moses led them away from their captors. God even parted the Red Sea to aid their escape.

You would think his people would praise him for such a long list of miracles on their behalf. You'd think they'd be grateful for their freedom as well as the gold they'd received from their former masters.

Instead, the Israelites grumbled and complained. They said, "Why have you brought us up out of Egypt to die in the desert? There is no bread! There is no water! And we detest this miserable food!" (Num. 21:5).

God was not pleased with his people. They refused to trust him or appreciate what he'd done for them. Therefore, God allowed fiery snakes to come out of the desert. The people who were bitten by snakes died.

The lesson to us? Just as the bite from a fiery snake meant death, the bite of sin also means death. Yet, it was there in that snake-infested desert that God, the master of foreshadowing, provided an illustration of how he would provide salvation.

"The LORD said to Moses, 'Make a snake and put it up on a pole; anyone who is bitten can look at it and live.' So Moses made a bronze snake and put it up on a pole. Then when anyone was bitten by a snake and looked at the bronze snake, he lived" (Num. 21:8–9).

The lifting of the snake foreshadows the lifting up of Christ on the cross. The snake represents sin and Christ became *our* sin. If we look to him and believe, we are saved from the poison of sin and death. John 3:14–15 says, "Just as Moses lifted up the snake in the desert, so the Son of Man must be lifted up, that everyone who believes in him may have eternal life."

Who do we look to for our salvation? We look to Jesus, raised up on the cross, and then raised up from the dead. Imagine his great love for us. Jesus, God's royal Son, loved us so much he allowed himself to be born a babe in a manger. He allowed himself to be tied to the pains of this earth as he grew to become a young man with a destiny. He was the chosen one who came to set us free from sin and death.

Jesus allowed himself, God's only begotten Son, to be led to the cross and hung until he was dead. At the moment Jesus passed from the land of the living, even the rocks cried out! The ground shook and darkness covered the earth. It was the darkest hour in the history of both heaven and earth; so dark that even God couldn't watch. At this moment God's own Son entered into death. How Satan must have gloried in his victory. He thought he'd won his battle against heaven at long last.

How wrong he was. Little did Lucifer know that Jesus' tomb was only a passageway from death to life! Satan, that old serpent from the Garden of Eden, had been thwarted by the cross, the weapon he thought brought his victory. But the cross was actually the weapon of his defeat; it sealed his doom.

Satan celebrated for the three days Jesus' body lay in a cave-like tomb. But on the third day, Satan's demonic victory party came to an abrupt end. Rays of glory spilled through the cracks of the tomb's sealed doorway as Christ's spirit ignited his crucified body.

The earth shook as Christ rose from his pallet. Bound in strips of burial cloth, he pulled away his bonds. The tomb shuddered as an angel rolled back the stone that had covered the entrance. Then, in the hush of morning, while all of heaven held its breath, Christ placed a nail-pierced foot onto the dew-covered grass. The Son rose with the glory of the sunrise! Not even the fiery orb of the sun could compare with the holy glow of Christ's face. Christ Jesus had risen! He was the answer to the divine question! And now, two thousand years later, Satan is still defeated and the choir of heaven still rejoices!

It's not enough to know about God's great love for us, or the sacrifice Jesus made for us. We still need forgiveness of our sins. No matter how good we are, the poison of sin runs in our very veins. Unless we get the antidote, we'll surely die.

> Christ Jesus had risen! He was the answer to the divine question! And now, two thousand years later, Satan is still defeated and the choir of heaven still rejoices!

Once, while I was on a ride-along with a Texas policeman, we were called to a Corpus Christi grocery store where the manager had apprehended two teenage girls for eating donuts in the checkout line. It turned out the girls didn't have as much money as they'd thought. They were a quarter short of paying their bill. The manager demanded their arrest.

That's exactly what Lucifer demands. He's our accuser, and whether we have lived our lives shamefully or have come in only a quarter short of perfection, he demands justice. He demands our execution, our continued separation from God.

Though we don't deserve it, our big brother, Jesus, stands before the throne of God saying, "I know this one. This one looks to me for salvation. I took the punishment in this one's stead. Unlock the chains. This debt has been paid in full."

Let that realization sink in. Then offer a prayer of praise to God.

Perhaps you've never made the choice to become a follower of Christ. You can right now. Perhaps you've already accepted the sacrifice Jesus has made for your sins, but even so, let's all pray the following prayer together to reaffirm our belief.

Dear Father,

Thank you for sending Jesus to die in my place. I believe he took my sin upon himself and took my punishment on the cross. I believe that through his death and resurrection, he defeated sin.

I once and for all place my sin on him.

Father, please forgive me for these sins. I turn from my sins and commit to live my life for you. Please fill me with your precious spirit, and give me your power to live my life for you.

In the wonderful name of Jesus,

Amen.

Okay, take a moment to thank God! Dance around the room if you feel like it, but tell God how much you love him and thank him for what he has done for you.

Wow and hallelujah!

Now for the rest of the story. Your story starts when you look to Jesus on the cross. But there's something else you need to know so you can effectively pray for yourself.

You now have a new identity. The old you has died, and a new you has raised from the ashes. Maybe it's time to look in God's mirror to see who you have become.

James 1:23–25 reminds us how important it is to look at and live our lives from God's perspective, and by doing so, we'll be blessed.

Anyone who listens to the word but does not do what it says is like a man who looks at his face in a mirror and, after looking at himself, goes away and immediately forgets what he looks like. But the man who looks intently into the perfect law that gives freedom, and continues to do this, not forgetting what he has heard, but doing it—he will be blessed in what he does.

Now you know God loves you, that Jesus, his Son, died for your sins so that you can be forgiven and draw closer to God. This knowledge helps you to know it's okay to pray for yourself. But before we go any further with the concept of self-prayer, let's look a little deeper into God's mirror.

Knowing Who You Are in Christ

Not long ago, I watched a simply delightful made-for-TV movie called *The Inheritance*, a work based on a novelette written by Louisa May Alcott (the author of *Little Women*) when she was only seventeen years old.

In this charming period piece written in 1849, a young woman named Edith works as a servant for the wealthy Hamilton family as a companion to the Hamiltons' lovely daughter, Amy. Though the beloved Edith has been with the family since she was a baby, she has no rights, privileges, or share in the family's wealth or social standing.

This realization becomes tragic when Edith falls in love with a wealthy young man named James Percy. She realizes that a match between her, a lowly servant, and James, would hurt his future career and standing in society. Therefore she believes she has no right to be by his side.

Out of love for James, Edith turns her back on a chance for true love. That is, until she discovers her real identity, an identity that had been unknown by either herself or the Hamiltons. Edith learns she's not the child of a servant who died in childbirth, as had been thought. She's actually the orphaned daughter of Mr. Hamilton's brother and his secret wife. Edith discovers that instead of being a servant, she's actually Mr. Hamilton's niece, Amy's cousin—family!

This truth brings an inheritance of wealth, class, social standing, and the right to marry the man of her dreams. Her new identity changed everything.

This story reminds me of your story. You are not a ragged servant of the king; instead you are his child through the work of Christ. Christ has given you an inheritance and a robe of righteousness to wear. Therefore, walk in the joy of who you are in him.

> As you study and come to understand who you are, you will discover that the truth of your new identity in Christ will change everything.

As you study and come to understand who you are, you will discover that the truth of your new identity in Christ will change everything.

When you don't know who you are in Christ, you may miss all the benefits God has made available to you. You need to check your inheritance policy (it's found in the pages of your Bible). I happen to have an abbreviated version for you to review below. I've paraphrased several references, which you may want to look up later. I've designed this paraphrased version of your policy to be read *aloud* to yourself before God.

I am:

Born again. Through the work of Jesus on the cross, I have been made new (2 Cor. 5:17).

Forgiven. Through Christ's death on the cross, God has forgiven my sins (Eph. 1:7).

Not bound by sin. I am free because Jesus was raised from the dead. My old self was crucified with him (Rom. 6:4–8).

The righteousness of Christ. Jesus, who was innocent, became sin and was punished so I could claim his righteousness (2 Cor. 5:21).

Not alone. At Jesus' request, God has sent me his Holy Spirit to be my counselor. His spirit of truth lives within me (John 14:16–18).

Holy. I am holy through the sacrifice of Jesus Christ (Heb. 10:10).

Right with God. Because I believe and receive the work of Jesus, God has accepted me (Rom. 3:21–24).

At peace with God. Because God justifies me through faith (Rom. 5:1).

God's friend. God's name for me is not "servant" but "friend" (John 15:15).

Blessed. God has given me every spiritual blessing in Christ (Eph. 1:3).

Strong. God gives me strength (1 Cor. 1:8).

Victorious over the evil one. I have God's strength to turn from my sin, and because Jesus is holding on to me securely, the devil cannot get his hands on me (1 John 5:18).

God's possession. God has purchased me and he plans on keeping me for himself (Eph. 1:14).

Shielded by God's power. God shields me because I trust him (1 Peter 1:5).

God's beloved. God loves me and I love God (John 14:21).

To bear fruit. God picked me to do a work that will bear lasting fruit for his kingdom (John 15:16).

You've got to be impressed with the new you. Knowing who you are in Christ frees you to be and do what he's called you to be and do. It helps you see your worth to God through Christ so that, among other things, you can have the confidence to pray for yourself.

Some people find it helps to repeat these attributes aloud daily to remind them that their old nature has passed on and the new nature has arrived and is ready to live for Christ.

Romans 6:5–7 puts it this way: "For if we have been planted together in the likeness of his death, we shall be also in the likeness of his resurrection: Knowing this, that our old man is crucified with him, that the body of sin might be destroyed, that henceforth we should not serve sin. For he that is dead is freed from sin" (KJV).

The Prayer Christ Prayed for Us

Another reason to pray for yourself is because Jesus prays for you. He is before the throne, making intercession for you to the Father (see Rom. 8:34). If Jesus would pray for you, then you should follow his example and join him.

The Bible records a remarkable prayer that Jesus prayed on our behalf. It's found in John 17:1–26, and I encourage you to read it in its entirety for yourself. If we look at what Jesus prayed for us, we'll discover how to pray for ourselves (as well as how to live for Christ).

It was a dark night in the Garden of Gethsemane, and the hour was late. In just a few hours Jesus would be arrested, leading to his trial and crucifixion. Jesus had called his disciples to pray with him as he waited for Judas, the one who would soon betray him. Jesus knew this was his closing benediction with his disciples, and what he prayed for them he meant for each one of us. Before we examine this prayer, take a moment now to ask the Lord to open your understanding.

> My prayer is not for [the disciples] alone. I pray also for those who will believe in me through their message, that all of them may be one, Father, just as you are in me and I am in you. May they also be in us so that the world may believe that you have sent me. I have given them the glory that you gave me, that they may be one as we are one: I in them and you in me. May they be brought to complete unity to let the world know that you sent me and have loved them even as you have loved me.
>
> Father, I want those you have given me to be with me where I am, and to see my glory, the glory you have given me because you loved me before the creation of the world.
>
> Righteous Father, though the world does not know you, I know you, and they know that you have sent me. I have made you known to them, and will continue to make you known in order that the love you have for me may be in them and that I myself may be in them.
>
> John 17:20–26

Let's go over the highlights of the complete prayer in John 17:1–26. Jesus prayed that we would find joy as we understand his requests to God on our behalf. Jesus prayed that we would:

- Have eternal life so we may know both God and his Son (v. 3).
- Have knowledge that we belong to Jesus and therefore to God (v. 6).
- Be protected and safe from the evil one (v. 15).
- Be sanctified by the truth of God's Word as we are sent into the world (vv. 17–18).

- Have unity among believers, just as the Father is in Jesus and Jesus is within us (v. 21).
- Have belief that God sent Jesus (v. 21).
- Have complete unity so the world may know God sent Jesus and that God loves us even as he loves his Son (v. 23).
- Be with Jesus and see his glory, the glory God gave him before the beginning of the world (v. 24).
- Understand that God's love may be in us as it is within Jesus (v. 26).

What a wonderful prayer Jesus prayed for us. May we all pray in agreement:

> Lord, we agree with these requests that Jesus prayed on our behalf. Thank you, Father, for loving us and allowing Jesus to be in us as you are in us. Help us to live in love and unity with you, him, and one another so the world will recognize Jesus and you.

Now, stay with me as we move into the final and most important part of this chapter: powerful prayers that you can pray for yourself. This is a good opportunity to focus on your relationship with God.

How to Pray for Yourself

We read the Lord's Prayer often enough, but sometimes we miss out on his words of instruction at the beginning of that prayer. Jesus said,

> And when you pray, do not be like the hypocrites, for they love to pray standing in the synagogues and on the street corners

to be seen by men. I tell you the truth, they have received their reward in full. But when you pray, go into your room, close the door and pray to your Father, who is unseen. Then your Father, who sees what is done in secret, will reward you. And when you pray, do not keep on babbling like pagans, for they think they will be heard because of their many words. Do not be like them, for your Father knows what you need before you ask him.

Matthew 6:5–8

These are great instructions and now it's time to follow them with prayers I affectionately refer to as "give me" prayers.

No, it's not wrong to ask God to give you things. Later in this book, we'll talk about how God might answer your prayers.

Ready to pray? It's not difficult. All you have to do is read the following prayers (as based on paraphrased Scripture) aloud or in the stillness of your heart. Either way, God will hear you.

Dear Father:

I pray that I would *know you more* than ever before.

As the psalmist wrote, I pray that I would have *victory* in the struggles I'm facing or will face. (See Ps. 44:7.)

I pray for *healing* and good *health*, just as King Hezekiah prayed. (See 2 Kings 20:5.)

I pray for godly *wisdom*, just as King Solomon prayed. (See 2 Chron. 1:10.)

Like the sons of Reuben, the Gadites, half the tribe of Manasseh, and many of the kings of Israel, I pray for *strength* for the battles I will face and perseverance as I journey through life. (See 1 Chron. 5:20.)

And just as you gave Moses instruction, I pray for *anointed direction* in my steps and that you will be with me on this journey you have given me. (See Exod. 24:12.)

Like Jabez, I pray for *blessings*, gifts from you, in my life. (See 1 Chron. 4:10.)

Like Paul, I pray for *hope* so that I may not lose heart. (See Rom. 12:12.)

Like King David, I pray for *courage* and *protection* over my house or life and family. (See 2 Sam. 7:27–29.)

As Paul and Timothy taught, I pray for *financial* prosperity and provision for all my *needs*. (See Phil. 4:19.)

As David prayed for a revelation of your will, I pray that I would recognize and take the *opportunities* you provide, but help me not to pry open doors you have closed. (See Ps. 143:10.)

Like the voice that called from the throne of God, I pray that I would understand how *wonderful*, *awesome*, and *greatly to be praised* you are. (See Rev. 19:5.)

I humbly submit these requests and thank you, Lord, for hearing my prayer. I lay these requests at your feet. I love you so much. Thank you for the privilege of being your beloved child.

In the name of Jesus, whom I love,

Amen.

In addition to these prayers for health, wisdom, and finances, you can include prayers about the details of your life. Continue your time of prayer, adding details about the situations, heartaches, and concerns you are facing today. The following prayer provides a format that you can follow as you pray, but feel free to pray as you feel the Holy Spirit leading you.

Dear Lord,

First, please forgive me of my sins. I come to you, not in my righteousness, but in the righteousness of your Son, Jesus. I come to you because I am concerned about _____. Please shine the light of your love and wisdom into this situation regarding _____. Show me how you want me to respond.

I ask that you change _____ or change my heart regarding this matter. Heal the things that need to be healed, teach me the lessons you want me to learn, give me the ability to show your love and light in this situation. I take authority and bind the work of the enemy from this situation in Jesus' name and in the power of his blood and resurrection.

Lord, I ask that your will be done and that you give me eyes to see you at work, that you give me a heart to love and to forgive. Thank you, Father, that you are on the move, bringing good out of this situation. I trust you and I praise you.

In Jesus' name,

Amen.

It's okay to become your own prayer project because praying for yourself is not about getting or hoarding blessings. Rather, it's about taking the hand of Jesus and confidently walking with him. This is not about getting your way or checking the answered prayers off your request list. It's about going deeper in your relationship with Christ. Be assured that what God desires most is friendship with you. Perhaps you find this shocking. The King of the universe wants to be friends? Wants a deeper friendship with whom? Me?

Yes. And that's the real secret of prayer—going deeper into a relationship with God.

Yes, there is still sin and suffering in the world, but Jesus is the answer who gives hope and life into each of these situations when he's invited into them.

In the following chapters, we are going deeper still. So, reach out for the hand of your brother Jesus. He wants to take you places you've never been before. Join me for the adventure of a lifetime including the next phase of our prayer project as you learn to pray in a way to help you realize God's presence.

4

What to Pray to Help You Realize God's Presence

A believer longs after God—to come into His presence—to feel His love—to feel near to Him in secret—to feel in the crowd that he is nearer than all the creatures. Ah! dear brethren, have you ever tasted this blessedness? There is greater rest and solace to be found in the presence of God for one hour, than in an eternity of the presence of man.

—Robert Murray M'Cheyne

Not long ago, I got an email that said,

Dear Linda,
I've tried, but I just can't feel God's presence. Can you help me?
—Lonely for God[1]

I wrote back:

Dear Lonely for God,
Our spiritual journey is a lot like driving your car while listening to the radio. Imagine what it would be like to tune

the radio to your favorite station, then a few miles down the road suddenly lose the signal. Sometimes our relationship with God seems to be like that. Sometimes we hear his voice (or signal) clearly in our lives. At other times, he seems silent. His silence can mean one of two things:

We've tuned in to a different station and can't hear his voice. (Though he never stops loving us.)

We're experiencing a quiet phase of not hearing God's voice in order to develop our faith and to prepare our hearts to be right with him.

I've experienced both situations myself. Sometimes I hear God's voice loud and clear. He speaks and I feel his sweet presence. Other times, I've run ahead of God or taken a path he hasn't meant for me and I have to turn around to see where he is.

Then there are times God wants me to *wait* on him. He wants me to believe and *wait* until he feels I'm ready to hear his voice. That happens when God wants me to grow in my faith, to believe in him, even when I'm not sure of his presence.

Linda

We Live by Faith Not Sight

There are times we can't hear God's voice or feel his presence. That's when we have to continue our relationship with God on faith. Dictionary.com defines faith as, "Belief that does not rest on logical proof or material evidence."

For as Paul said, "We live by faith, not by sight" (2 Cor. 5:7).

This may not be the best news for those of us who wish God would hand over an entire map of our future with footnotes to clearly explain our current crisis. But perhaps the real point is we need to develop such a deep relationship with

God that we can completely trust him with our problems as well as with our future. We need to find that place where like Job, a godly man who suffered many heartaches and tragedies, we can say, "Though he slay me, yet will I hope in him" (Job 13:15).

And that's our goal: to trust God with our current circumstances as well as our life's journeys because we know all things work for the good of those who love him and are called to his purpose (see Rom. 8:28).

Reasons Why God May Feel Far Away

There are several reasons why one may not feel God's presence, including:

- Lack of invitation
- Unanswered prayer
- Sin
- Grief
- Not understanding the depth of God's love

Lack of Invitation

I sometimes host a Christian TV program in Denver. Recently I had a delightful guest named Pastor Rene' Whitmore. Pastor Rene' and her husband David are pastors of Spread the Word Full Gospel Church in Denver.

Rene' and I had an astounding time, live, on the Denver airways. As I was introducing her and just before she sang her song, "Come Holy Spirit," I said to the camera, "We have two special guests today. One is Pastor Rene' Whitmore and the other is the Lord and his precious Holy Spirit. In fact, we've invited him to be on our program today and we are inviting him to join you in your home or wherever you are."

Moments later, as Rene' began to sing, his presence began to move.

Suddenly the station's phones began to ring off the wall. The lines were absolutely jammed with people calling in for prayer, for rededication, and to commit their lives to Christ.

I was astounded.

Now, I'm not saying that Rene', my guest, wasn't anointed. She certainly was. But I am saying this was the first time I'd publicly invited the Lord to join us on set and in the homes of our viewers. There was no doubt he accepted the invitation.

> What would happen if we extended a special invitation to the Lord and his Holy Spirit to join us in our lives, our homes, our churches, our communities, and our workplaces?

That leads me to ask a question: what would happen if we extended a special invitation to the Lord and his Holy Spirit to join us in our lives, our homes, our churches, our communities, and our workplaces?

Could it be the Lord is still waiting to receive such an invitation from us? Okay, I'm convicted, and I think we ought to pray about this together, right now. Whisper this prayer with me:

Dear Lord,

I apologize to you for leaving you off my guest list in my life, my home, my church, my community, my relationships, and my workplace. Forgive me.

Lord, this is a special invitation I'm extending to you to come and join me in all areas and relationships of my life.

First, Lord, you are invited to join me in my thoughts, prayer, and quiet time.

Second, you are invited to join me in my home, family, and friends.

Please, Lord, come to my church. Come to my workplace, my friendships and relationships, and my neighborhood and community.

You and your Holy Spirit are invited and welcome to move into every area of my life.

Come, Lord; come, Jesus; come, Holy Spirit. Come.

In the name of Jesus,

Amen.

I'm convinced that God will respond to this invitation especially as we start to pray it at meals, at work, at school, at church, at weddings and funerals, and at the beginning of each new day.

When we invite God to join us, we must be sure to entertain his presence.

Otherwise, our invitation could end up like the strange lunch date I once had with my husband, Paul. You see, Paul had phoned to invite me to join him for lunch at our favorite restaurant. Of course, I cheerfully said yes to a date with my sweetie.

> When we invite God to join us, we must be sure to entertain his presence.

I hurried down to the restaurant and told the waiter that my husband would soon join me. I had the waiter seat me at a table where I could watch the entrance.

I ordered two iced teas with lemon and waited. Paul never walked through the door. Finally, I dug my cell phone out of my purse and called his office.

No answer.

After waiting an hour, I paid for the iced teas and went home.

Once there, I tried his office again. This time he picked up.

"Paul, where were you?" I asked.

"I was at the restaurant. Where were you?"

"I was at the restaurant too."

Soon it became clear the waiter had seated us back to back. We'd had lunch together but hadn't known it. I think that's what is happening in our churches, our families, and our communities. We might invite God to join us, but then we pay little attention to him once he arrives. We somehow turn our backs on God, looking everywhere except to the one who should have our undivided attention.

> If you can't feel God's presence, perhaps you need to turn around to see where he is. You may be surprised to discover he's never left your side. The only thing missing is your attention and focus on him.

If you can't feel God's presence, perhaps you need to turn around to see where he is. You may be surprised to discover he's never left your side. The only thing missing is your attention and focus on him.

When you invite him to join you, invite him to lead you. Then, if you ever discover you made the wrong turn, turn around. Be assured if you are trying to walk in his will, he will never let you out of his sight.

So, stop letting fear keep you from doing those things he's called you to do. And remember, if you ever run ahead of God, you can't run so far that he can't get you back on track.

Unanswered Prayer

I hear about the problem of unanswered prayer a lot. There's nothing like feeling "rejected" in your prayer life. There's nothing as tragic as one who believes all hope is gone because God doesn't seem to care.

If you've been tempted to fret about unanswered prayer, perhaps it's not that God has rejected you, but rather that you're suffering from "feelings of rejection" because God has not come through the way you've insisted. Perhaps a change of perspective is in order.

Think about that as you read Sheila's story . . .

The seriousness of Sheila's blue eyes caught me off guard. "I want to talk to you in private," she said. "I think you may be the only person who can understand what I'm going through."

On the surface, the waves were stormy, but it was in the cool peaceful depths where God was working—the depths where I couldn't see.

We slipped out of the conference we were attending and into an empty classroom. Sheila said, "I have a teenage daughter who is mentally ill. And I've done everything I can to help her, but she's not getting better, instead, she's getting worse—more violent. I've prayed and prayed, but I feel like my prayers are hitting the ceiling. I still consider myself a Christian, but it seems as if God is for everyone else, but he's not for me."

I touched my friend's hand. "I've been there, Sheila. When Laura spent a year in a coma, I too felt cut off from God."

"I knew you must have," Sheila confided.

I nodded. "What I've learned through my ordeal is that you can't go by appearances."

"What do you mean?"

"When Laura was in a coma, it seemed as if God was not to be found. But he was there. On the surface, the waves were stormy, but it was in the cool peaceful depths where God was working—the depths where I couldn't see. I thought God had deaf ears and Laura was going to stay in her coma forever.

But God was awakening her, even when I didn't realize he was at work."

"But God doesn't seem to be at work in our situation," Sheila complained. "Amy's tantrums are getting more violent. Plus, the kids at school call her 'retard.' Do you know what this does to her self-esteem? On top of that, Amy's medication is having bad side affects. She's more moody than ever. Because Christians often have a hard time understanding and dealing with mental illness, we're not getting a lot of support. Even Amy's teacher thinks my daughter's problems are my fault. Mrs. Smith says if my faith were stronger, God would heal her!"

"But Sheila, we can't hold a gun to God and demand that he do what we say because we claim we have enough faith. Instead, we have to trust him—to believe he is all powerful, powerful enough to heal Amy or powerful enough to help us through our struggles. This is what true faith is all about."

Sheila smiled. "Then I do have faith!"

I nodded. "If you believe in God's power, you have faith. Just don't accept false guilt, Sheila. You don't need it."

And that's the truth. We don't know the mind of God or understand his ways. Our perspective is so limited that we can't even imagine our life from heaven's viewpoint. Therefore, it's our job to give our burdens to the Lord in prayer, then to trust him with the results. We'll talk about this very important issue again.

Sin

Years ago, I had an online instant message conversation with a teenager. He IM-ed me, "I can't feel God's presence anymore, and I can't figure out why."

As I used to be a youth director, I had some ideas as to what the problem might be, so I wrote, "Do you take drugs?"

"Yes," he said. "I'm in a gang, and I'm both a user and a pusher."

I typed back, "I think I see the problem."

He typed back, "What? I don't get it."

He didn't get it? He wasn't entertaining God, he was entertaining sin. That's like putting cotton in our spiritual ears and wondering why we can't hear God's voice.

> If we have sin in our lives, we need to clean up our act so we can enjoy his sweet spirit.

Oh, it's not like God quits loving us, it's more like we can't hear his music because we're tuned in to another station. We need to tune our antenna to God! We need to stop watching the shows we know we shouldn't see. Quit listening to the music we know we shouldn't hear. Quit saying those things about our pastor, our family, our spouse, our co-workers, and our neighbors that we know we shouldn't say. Stop sleeping with those people to whom we're not married. Block the porn sites. Stop with the drugs and the alcohol.

God hasn't moved. He hasn't left us. However, if we have sin in our lives, we need to clean up our act so we can enjoy his sweet spirit.

If we don't start taking our Christian walk more seriously, we're going to reap disaster in our personal lives, our families, our churches, and our community. Why? Because when we go our own way we'll zoom headlong into trouble. So, if you're doing something you shouldn't, stop it, right now. Put it down or turn it off and walk away.

Grief

Grief is a temporary reason why it can be difficult to hear God's voice.

I just talked this over with a friend who is grieving over one of her children who continues to make devastating choices.

Between sobs, Alisha said, "I just can't feel God's presence. There must be something wrong with me."

"There is," I said, giving her a hug. "You have a broken heart, and God understands that. This situation with your child hurts so much that you feel spiritually numb. But that doesn't mean God's not with you. The Word says he is near the brokenhearted. But his presence is something you're going to have to take on faith in this difficult season of your life."

Friends, there's something about heartache that seems to interfere with our "God radar." I think it's because grief can overwhelm us to the point that we have a limited capacity to see or feel anything outside our emotional trauma. This reaction to grief is only human, but there are things you can do to overcome.

1. Recognize you are in deep pain.
2. Give your pain as an offering to God. (This may be something you have to do repeatedly.)
3. Take it on faith that God hasn't forgotten you or abandoned you.

In time, you will hear God's voice again and feel his presence, just like my friend Kathy.

Kathy said, "My mother came from strong Nebraskan stock. She and Dad owned a ranch and she was always bustling about." Her face darkened. "Recently, when she was on a trip visiting me, she had a massive stroke that affected her brain stem. I sat by her hospital bed and cried. My mom couldn't even open her eyes. It was so hard to see this strong woman so helpless."

Kathy paused, pain glistening in her eyes.

"One of my friends brought me a beautifully wrapped box. Inside I found an afghan with a card that read, 'Remember when you're all alone, your loving heavenly Father is there to wrap his arms around you. Wrap yourself in this blanket and know that you are wrapped in his love.'"

Kathy told me, "Whenever I felt afraid or lonely, I wrapped myself in that afghan and knew God was with me." Her voice quivered. "I spent so much time wrapped in that blanket, sitting near my mother's bed. It was so meaningful to realize I was wrapped in God's love."

If you're grieving, I want you to stop and picture this blanket of love wrapped around you. It's there; all you need to do is to realize it by praying,

Dear Lord,
Because of the pain in my heart, it's been hard to feel your presence. Help me to know you are with me and that your love surrounds me. Wrap me in your love, break through my pain and carry it for me.
In Jesus' name,
Amen.

Not Understanding the Depth of God's Love

And speaking of understanding God's love, that understanding is key to helping us develop our prayer life. Yet, understanding God's love is something we believers often struggle with.

Let's see if I can paint a picture of God's love for you through this charming fairy tale. Roll the tape . . .

Once upon a time there was a poor and not-so-lovely princess in love with the great prince. She decided to go on a quest to find beauty and to win her fortune so she could win his love.

On the first day of her journey she came upon a poor blind lad who'd lost his way. Time was of the essence, and if she stopped to help the child she would be delayed from her mission. Nevertheless, the princess led the boy back to his grateful mother. As she was leaving, the lad's mother said, "Thank you, Princess, you have such a beautiful heart!"

The princess traveled on and soon heard the sound of weeping. There on the side of the road sat a little girl. "What is wrong?" the princess asked the child.

"I'm hungry," the girl said. "I have no coin to buy my dinner."

The princess opened her purse and looked at her meager means. She looked up and smiled. "Then I have good news," she told the girl. "I have enough to not only buy my dinner but yours as well."

> Stop and ask God to show you how great and high his love is for you. Once you realize this truth, you will break through to experience deepest joy and more meaningful times of prayer.

As the grateful child, coin in hand, skipped down the road to the market, the prince stepped from the wood. He called, "Princess, my love."

The princess turned from him. "Do you not see that I am neither lovely nor wealthy? I do not deserve your love."

The prince replied, "But my princess, you have a beauty in your heart that will never fade. You have riches enough to share with others. You are my love!"

Do you get it? Like the prince in this story, Jesus the Great Prince loves us despite our shortcomings. We'll never be beautiful enough, perfect enough, good enough, rich enough, or pure enough to deserve his love. But somehow he sees something in us that we can't see ourselves. Somehow he sees us as worthy of his love. He sees us as lovable!

Stop and ask God to show you how great and high his love is for you. Once you realize this truth, you will break through to experience deepest joy and more meaningful times of prayer.

Praying Scripture

In the previous chapter, we had the opportunity to pray through a few Scriptures. This can be a very powerful form of prayer because you are essentially agreeing with the Word of God.

Let's try it again, with these paraphrased Scriptures . . .

Dear Lord, I agree that I am . . .

- *In your presence*—because where can I go from your spirit or flee from your presence? You are with me. (See Ps. 139:7.)
- *Your temple*—because your spirit lives in me. (See 1 Cor. 3:16.)
- *Loved by you*—because you showed your great love for me by sending Christ to die for me, while I was still a sinner. (See Rom. 5:6–8.)
- *Chosen by you*—because long ago, even before you made the world, you chose me to be your very own. Through Christ, I am holy in your eyes. Because I am covered by your love, you see me without a single fault. (See Eph. 1:4, 11–12.)

Our Silent Prayer Retreat

Would you like to take a private prayer retreat with Jesus?

Read these instructions and then try it.

To go on a silent prayer retreat, close your eyes, lean your head slightly to the left or to the right, then imagine that you are leaning your head on the Lord's shoulder.

Of course, this symbolic act is just a way to help you invite the presence of the Lord into this moment.

Now, before you leave for your retreat to spend some time abiding with the Lord, know I'll be waiting for you when you get back, with great news about how to pray when life is overwhelming.

See you soon. Oh, while you're spending time with the Lord, be sure to tell him you love him and allow yourself to rest in his great love for you.

5

What to Pray
When Your Burdens Are Heavy

Pray and let God worry.
—Martin Luther

Times of trouble give us a lot of motivation to learn how to pray. Sometimes falling on our knees is the only way to learn how to stand. Even so, trouble should not be our only motivation to talk to God. Andrew Murray (1828–1917), a pastor and missionary to South Africa, once said, "Some people pray just to pray and some people pray to know God."[1]

At times, trouble can send us running to God. And if that's the case for you, trouble has already given you a divine benefit.

Nevertheless, those of us who have been up to our necks in both natural and man-made disaster know trouble is not the preferred place to be. However, just like hot water can brew a strong cup of tea, being steeped in hot water can make us strong as well. But know if you are feeling overwhelmed, you're not alone. In fact, many visitors to GodTest.com drop by because they too are feeling overwhelmed. One such visitor wrote:

I'm in over my head. I see no way out of my situation. I've cried out to God, but I'm getting nowhere. I need answers and I need them now. I don't know how much longer I can hold on.[2]

Here's my reply:

Oh, Dear One,

Here's a better solution: seek God's direction. When you do, he'll guide you one step at a time. And when you trust God, you'll discover that solutions never arrive early but just in time.

There was once a mother of four teenagers whose husband died suddenly. She didn't know how she was going to make it. She was so depressed, all she could do was sit on the couch and cry. One day, she prayed, "Jesus, if you were here, what would you have me do?"

She was surprised when she heard a gentle whisper in her heart. He said, "Get up and do the dishes."

She did. Then for the first time in a long time, she made dinner for her kids. She just kept doing the next thing until she saw all of her kids successfully graduate from high school.

I think you're in a place similar to the one this distraught mother experienced. If you look at your whole situation and your hurts all at once, you'll feel overwhelmed. But Jesus is whispering to you, "Seek me. And do the next thing." Get up, do the next thing, and the next, and the next. Live your life!

You can't control the people and situations in your life, but you can take these people and situations to God and give them to him along with all your past hurts.

Every day, say to God, "Lord, you say to cast my cares on you, so I'm throwing all these burdens on your shoulders.

Please carry them for me. I'm too tired to worry about them today. You do it."

Over time, your heart will start to feel lighter and you'll have clearer focus and direction. You'll start to enjoy life.

The Bible says, "Anyone who is among the living has hope—even a live dog is better off than a dead lion!" (Eccles. 9:4). That means there is no hope in death, but only in life. Even if you're feeling like a starving dog that everyone kicks around, at least you're alive, and your life is gifted with hope.

Wait. Wait on God. In the meantime, if thoughts of suicide get too heavy, go to the hospital or call 911. Call your doctor for a checkup.

Your friend,

Linda

Letting Go through Prayer

One of the best benefits we can receive from a prayer life is learning to let go. In fact, I think prayer is really the process of letting go. You are letting go by taking your burdens and giving them to God.

> I think prayer is really the process of letting go. You are letting go by taking your burdens and giving them to God.

The sooner we learn we're not in control of our lives, situations, or heartaches, the sooner we'll learn to trust God on a deeper level. After all, our lives are in his hands not our own.

One of the first times I ever realized prayer was essentially telling God, "It's not up to me, it's up to you," was as a nineteen-year-old college student at Lamar University in Beaumont, Texas.

That summer I'd been sent out by Texas Baptists to the town of La Pryor, Texas, to serve as a youth director.

La Pryor, a small farming town between San Antonio and the border of Mexico, seemed to attract drug smugglers. The kids I worked with often pointed them out to me whenever they drove past the church.

One day, when we were in the safety of our small church classroom, I suggested to the kids, "Let's pray for a miracle. Let's dream up a prayer that seems too big even for God and see what he does with it."

Veronica, a tiny teenager with dark brown hair and eyes to match, raised her hand. "You've been teaching us how to tell people about Jesus," she said. "Let's pray God will give us the chance to witness to our town's gang members!"

I gulped. Honestly, that was the last thing I wanted to pray, but how could I back out now? "All right," I said. "Why not? Let's pray we'll get a chance to witness to the town's gang members."

The young people bowed their heads and prayed earnestly. Despite our prayer request, I felt safe. These tough teens we were praying for were not likely to poke their heads around our church. And I wasn't likely to see them on the street. *Although*, I thought, *maybe one of my teens will get a chance to talk to them in the safety of the local market.*

The summer flew by. A few days before I was to return home, Rachel, another nineteen-year-old, joined me from Mexico. She'd come to help lead a Vacation Bible School at the Spanish church across town. We ended a wonderful week with a rousing parents' night. We stood by proudly as our young charges sang and signed "Jesus Loves Me" in American Sign Language.

Afterward, the stars above the West Texas town twinkled in a cloudless sky as Rachel and I waited in the deserted parking lot for the elderly pastor to drive us home. I noticed two teen boys walking toward the church. As they approached, the streetlight broke the shadows to reveal their faces. My heart pounded—it couldn't be. The faces belonged to two of the teen drug runners my youth group had been praying for.

This could mean trouble, I realized as I watched the boys approach. I turned to Rachel and whispered, "These boys are dangerous. Don't talk, don't breathe, and maybe they'll pass us by."

We stood as still as statues and were relieved when the boys passed us. Seconds later, they turned around.

"Hey, Linda!" a drunken voice called out.

Bad sign. They'd been drinking and they knew my name even though we'd never been introduced!

"What do you want?" I called into the darkness.

"Come over here!"

Rachel shouted back, "No, you come over here, under the light."

The two young men approached. Even in the dimness of the streetlight, I could see hate in their bloodshot eyes.

"What do you want?" I called again, trying to sound calm.

One of them, whom I later learned was Jose, stepped toward me, crowding me with his alcoholic breath. I stepped back, trying to escape the fumes.

"What do we want?" Jose slurred. "We want you to prove God is real!"

I swallowed hard. My voice sounded as if it belonged to a squeaky cartoon character. "God loves you. I know he's real. His Son Jesus died on the cross for you and provided forgiveness for your sins."

Jose sneered. "I don't want you to tell me about God. I want you to prove to me that he's real." He stepped even closer.

I again retreated, my back against a wall. "I can only prove it by telling you he's in my heart."

As Jose towered over me, his voice shook with anger. "That's not good enough. We want you to prove there's a God and we want you to prove it *now*!"

I glanced around nervously. There was nowhere to run and no one to help! *Lord*, I prayed, *there's nothing more I can say to these men to prove you are real. Would you please take over now? It's your turn.*

As I finished my silent prayer, the beautiful starry night changed. A strong wind rose as swirling dust pelted our faces.

> It's your turn.

High above our heads a cloud blotted out the stars. Jagged streaks of lightning broke the utter darkness, and thunder exploded the peace of the night.

Everyone froze as the wind pelted us with dirt and whipped our hair into our eyes. Rachel shouted above the great booms of thunder, "See, that's God telling you he's real!"

The boys ran one way, and Rachel and I ran the other. A few moments later the cloud passed and calm returned. When Rachel and I got to the home we were staying in, we were still awed. We sat on our bed in the safety of our little bedroom and smiled at each other.

"You know," I said, repeating myself for the hundredth time, "that really was God. He really was there."

"Yes," Rachel agreed, nodding as if in a trance. "He was awesome!"

The excitement of our discovery of God's presence and intervention gave us a sleepless but joyful night. And I learned God is waiting for us to say, "I've done all I can do, Lord. It's your turn."

I wrote the following poem to commemorate this lesson:

It's Your Turn, Lord

I found my dream and held it tight,
And prayed for wings to give it flight.

But yet it stayed earthbound with me,
Because I did not set it free.

Although I held it to my heart,
Somehow it seemed to fall apart.
"Oh Lord," I cried unhappily.
"Why did you take my dream from me?"

"My child, your dream is incomplete,
Until you lay it at my feet.
Unless you give your dream to me,
It cannot find its destiny."

I knew I had to let it go,
For I had nothing left to show.
Until my dream was in his hand,
I could not see his plan so grand.

At last I saw what he could do,
He shaped my broken dream anew.
For dreams will never find reward,
Until we say, "It's your turn, Lord."[3]

The Rest of My Story

I left you, in chapter 1, with my little girl just waking up from a coma. That was certainly a joyful time but not the end of the story.

One year later I was pushing Laura through the halls of the hospital in her wheelchair. At every turn, we ran into those famous health care professionals who had insisted Laura would never awaken. Each time we saw one of these professionals, Laura would smile and practically shout, "Hi!"

One of the worst of the naysayers, a speech therapist, was so startled she declared, "My, Laura is vocalizing."

"Yes," I agreed. "She just told you hello."

There was no mistaking the change in Laura. That day, Laura's lead doctor had to admit, "Laura's no longer in a coma nor is she in a vegetative state. She's awake and alert."

That was one of the most satisfying days of my life, but my satisfaction was incomplete. Yes, Laura was out of that nasty coma, but she was still profoundly disabled. Her laundry list of disabilities read like a bad ending to a good novel. She was paralyzed from the neck down, partially blind, and still on life support. I wondered why God would only heal someone part way.

This was a question I often contemplated as I visited various healing services and read books on healing. I was determined to find out how to claim God's miraculous healing power for my daughter. One Bible teacher told me my daughter's healing was incomplete because I didn't have enough faith. "Oh, really?" I told him, "Fine, use your faith. I'll watch." Okay, I didn't really say that, but I should have in an effort to show him the foolishness of his words.

> Faith simply believes God is able.

Because, you see, I did have faith, faith enough to seek out people who prayed for the sick. And as one minister privately told me, "Faith simply believes God is able."

You see, I believed God was able. In fact, I was surprised Laura's complete healing hadn't happened already. Though I'd been to the best-known faith healers in the Christian world, there was no change in Laura's condition.

One rainy afternoon three years after the accident, I slipped into Laura's room armed with my Bible, praise tapes, and carefully written faith statements describing my goal of God healing my daughter's disabilities.

But after an hour of earnestly telling God how much I believed for my miracle, I hit the wall. I suddenly knew my three-year struggle to carefully craft my faith had been for nothing. I discovered I had no more strength left to believe. Tears threatened to blind me as I realized I'd fought with all my might and lost.

I kissed Laura's cheek and watched her eyelashes flutter open. The lump in my throat suddenly knotted in my stomach. I tried to continue, turning the thin pages of my Bible to yet another faith Scripture to read aloud. But the blurry print could not give me hope. Sighing, I shut the Bible. *God hasn't answered my prayers, and that means Laura's never going to get better,* I thought in anguish as the rain and wind blew against Laura's windowpane. *Our situation is hopeless.*

Later, feeling rejected by God, I hid in the darkness of my bedroom, curtains drawn against the cold, continuing drizzle. I realized my hope was lost, replaced with shattered dreams. "Lord," I prayed, "are you there? I need you to speak to me if you want me to continue in my hope. Please show me what to do."

That evening in church, the deep voice of my pastor softened as he said, "The Lord has shown me there is someone here tonight who has lost hope."

I froze in my seat as shivers raised goose bumps on my arms. The pastor's eyes searched the congregation as I tried to appear invisible. "God wants you to look up. He is with you and will restore your hope in him."

I was stunned. *The pastor's message is too close to my afternoon prayer to be a coincidence. Maybe God is with me.*

As I drove home, a full moon reflected on the wet roadway while my thoughts turned from myself to God. I began to see how I'd missed God's truth by placing my faith not in him but in the earthly vessel of myself. I'd worked to have faith in my faith! Like two index fingers trapped in a Chinese finger puzzle, I'd been held captive by trusting myself instead of trusting God!

I pulled my van into the stillness of my garage. Turning off the engine, I laid my head on the steering wheel. I was finally ready to pray the prayer that would change my life.

"Lord," I prayed, "I transfer all my faith from myself to you." In my mind's eye I could see Jesus' loving face as I handed him the limp body of my daughter. "Lord, she is yours," I prayed. "I am going to trust you with her future. My faith in you no longer depends upon her healing, for as in the words of Job, 'Though he slay me, yet will I trust in him.'"

Suddenly filled with calm, I realized I was freed from the responsibility of making God mind me. I no longer had to perfect my faith so God would do my bidding. It was now all up to him. And incredibly, I finally got the healing I'd longed for. It didn't happen in Laura's body—it happened in my heart.

My grief was gone—really gone. At long last I was free.

Tears well in my eyes as I write this, because this lesson was hard fought and hard earned. As I look back at the years that have passed since I prayed this prayer of surrender, I can say with certainty it was the turning point of my life. It's the reason I have joy today. It's the reason for the miracle of my life and my ministry.

> And incredibly, I finally got the healing I'd longed for. It didn't happen in Laura's body—it happened in my heart.

When I finally prayed my "letting go" prayer, it touched the heart of God, and in turn, the heart of God touched me.

Is it time for you to find freedom from your troubles? Is it time you really gave them up to God? He is saying to you today, "Look up. I am with you and I will restore your hope in me."

It's time for you to let go of your struggle and trust God. Among other things, you may need to let go of worry, sin, grief, regrets, not through your power but God's power. That power can only be reached through prayer, which I will demonstrate in the next few paragraphs.

When my son was five, he painted an elaborate picture of a fire-breathing dragon scorching a spider. He said sweetly, "Mom, I'd like to give this picture to my sister Laura."

"How nice," I said.

That's when Jimmy hesitated and looked up at me with his big blue eyes. "But Mom, what if this picture turns real before morning?"

I had to laugh because Jimmy had painted the perfect picture of worry. Worry sometimes looms in our imaginations as elaborate pictures that will never come true. Or will they?

Well, what if they do? We are traveling through this life with the Lord of the universe. He promises that all things work for the good of those who love him. Even if our worst fears touch our lives, we can be assured that he's still in control and he will transform the situation and cause good to come from it. Let's pray:

Dear Lord,

I've made a decision to trust you with my circumstances. I hand all control to you. I know that all things work together for the good of those who love you. Therefore, I'm willing to live through this difficulty, in your strength and in your power. I thank you that these very circumstances, which I've found difficult to bear, are being used by you for miracles beyond imagination. I give you my worry, regardless of how things look, feel, or seem. You decide the outcome. Thank you that this is now your problem to do with what you will.

In the name of Jesus,
Amen.

Now take a deep breath. You are now worry free. Of course, you're going to try to pick up some of these worries again and possibly add new ones to your collection. But know that you can repeat this prayer as often as necessary.

Consequences of Sin

We're back to that, are we?

Yep.

A few years ago as I stood on a pier on Redondo Beach in Southern California, some young boys throwing bread crumbs on the sand captured my attention. They also caught the attention of several seagulls that swarmed down to sample their good fortune. But what these seagulls (and I) didn't know was that these boys had a big brother who was buried in the sand beneath the bread crumbs. Suddenly, two hands shot out of the sand and grabbed the legs of a seagull. The boy sat up, holding on to his flapping prize. Happily, after a couple of minutes the boy let the bird go.

But that is not always the case with our mortal enemy, Satan. He knows just how to create a trail of crumbs to lure us to his trap, where he lays in wait for us. We sample the crumbs of sin, one by one, as we inch closer to danger. The next thing we know, the enemy has captured us.

Are you caught in such a trap? Is the enemy holding on to you and you just can't get away? Though there will be consequences for your actions, God has the power to set you free. Pray the following prayer:

Dear Lord,

I blew it. I followed my desires instead of your path of righteousness. I fell into the enemy's trap and he has me bound. Father, I call out to you in the name of your Son,

Jesus. I call out to you and ask you to set me free from the clutches of the evil one.

I'm sorry for doing wrong. Please forgive me. I receive your forgiveness and the righteousness of your Son. Lord, it's your turn. I surrender all to you: my sin, this situation, and even the consequences.

Satan, I am wearing the righteousness of my brother, Savior, and Lord, Jesus. I am covered by the power of his blood. I demand that you release me, in the power of his name and resurrection. I do not belong to you, for I was bought at a price.

To you, Lord, I say thank you for setting me free.
In Jesus' name,
Amen.

When You've Done All You Can

Make a list of everything you want the Lord to carry for you. This list could include fear, heartache, temptation, finances, situations, trauma, a loved one, or anything else that's on your heart. Then pray:

Lord,
I give you _____. I ask you to carry this for me. From now on, _____ is your problem. Father, it's your turn.
In Jesus' name,
Amen.

What to Do Next

While hiking in the mountains, I once heard a cougar scream near the trail I was on. I stopped and raised my hands above my head to appear as large as possible. I knew if I ran or crouched I might seem like prey. So I stood large and still. The attack never came, and after I waited a while, I was able to go on my way unharmed.

The Bible says in 1 Peter 5:8–9, "Be self-controlled and alert. Your enemy the devil prowls around like a roaring lion looking for someone to devour. Resist him, standing firm in the faith." Don't stray off God's path for your life. Stand firm and show the evil one that you will not fall prey to his attacks.

> Don't stray off God's path for your life. Stand firm and show the evil one that you will not fall prey to his attacks.

Begin by putting on the full armor of God, found in Ephesians 6:10–18:

> Finally, be strong in the Lord and in his mighty power. Put on the full armor of God so that you can take your stand against the devil's schemes. For our struggle is not against flesh and blood, but against the rulers, against the authorities, against the powers of this dark world and against the spiritual forces of evil in the heavenly realms. Therefore put on the full armor of God, so that when the day of evil comes, you may be able to stand your ground, and after you have done everything, to stand. Stand firm then, with the belt of truth buckled around your waist, with the breastplate of righteousness in place, and with your feet fitted with the readiness that comes from the gospel of peace. In addition to all this, take up the shield of faith, with which you can extinguish all the flaming arrows of the evil one. Take the helmet of salvation and the sword of the Spirit, which is the word of God. And pray in the Spirit on all occasions with all kinds of prayers and requests. With this in mind, be alert and always keep on praying for all the saints.

I'll be honest with you. Ever since I was a little girl I've been confused by this passage. After all, how does one put on the armor of God? What special thing does one have to obtain to do so? How does one go about finding a sword of the Spirit?

But now I understand. God is saying that we have to acknowledge him and who we are in him so we can be ready for anything that life or the enemy throws our way. Turn this Ephesians passage into a daily prayer:

Dear Lord,

Help me to be strong in you and in your mighty power. Help me step into my full armor that you have given me so I can stand against the enemy's schemes. I acknowledge that the battle, though invisible, is raging all around me. My enemies are the powers of this dark world and the forces of evil from hell.

As I have the full armor of God, I will be able to stand my ground when the day of evil comes. I will stand my ground even after I have done all I can. I will stand firm with God's truth fastened around my waist. I will stand firm with God's righteousness over my heart. My feet stand ready on the gospel of peace. In addition to all this, I know God is able, and that knowledge I wear as a shield of faith, which will extinguish all the flaming arrows of the evil one. I wear the salvation of God like a helmet and God's Word like a sword, ready to pray or quote Scripture as needed. As the Spirit that is in me moves me to pray, I will pray on all occasions with all kinds of prayers and requests. With this in mind, I stand alert as I pray for all those who believe and follow you, God.

In Jesus' name,
Amen.

What to Pick Up and Hold Tight—God's Love

Now I have something to say to those of you who are in a difficult place through no fault of your own. I am not implying that all situations are rooted in a crummy choice. But because this is not heaven, bad things happen here on this sad, old earth. Storms equal to the destructive force of Katrina may tear apart your world. If you should ever entertain heartache, remember God has not forgotten you. If you are overwhelmed by tragic circumstances, take some time to contemplate God's love for you. Search your memory for times when you saw God move on your behalf. Remember and know that he is with you even now. Pore over Scripture, especially the Psalms, to read God's love letter to you so your heart may be encouraged. But whatever you do, don't give up in times of difficulty. If you give up you will never see the miracle God is creating from your life.

> Don't give up in times of difficulty. If you give up you will never see the miracle God is creating from your life.

I'll remind you of God's love song to you until I'm confident you've learned the words. Once you feel his music, this love song can heal your broken heart and perhaps save your life.

Pastor and bestselling author Rick Warren has said, "Knowing and loving God is our greatest privilege, and being known and loved is God's greatest pleasure."[4]

This is a profound thought.

A few years back, a disabled woman named Terri Schiavo succumbed to a court order that she be executed by starvation. My daughter, Laura, is even more profoundly disabled than was Terri Schiavo, and Terri's death broke my heart.

The week after Terri died, I was speaking at a women's spring banquet in Parker, Colorado. As I was being introduced, the Lord unexpectedly whispered to my spirit. "Do you know why it gave me great pleasure to leave Laura here on this earth as a disabled person?"

"Why, Lord?" I silently questioned.

"It's because your love for your daughter is like my love for my people. There is nothing my people can do to earn or deserve my love. I love them for who they are, unconditionally."

"As your little Laura is on life support, partially blind and paralyzed from the neck down, there's nothing she can do to earn your love. She'll never write a book, or even have the ability to read one. She will never run a marathon or paint a picture, but even so, you love her with a profound and deep love. Your love for your daughter is a picture of the love I have for my children."

Tears sprang to my eyes as I saw the beauty of such love and as I felt the sweetness of the love of God for me, for us all.

Praying Scripture

To wrap up what we learned in this chapter, pray aloud through the following paraphrased Scriptures. Then stay tuned for the next chapter, which is about what to do and how to pray when, yikes, you've been betrayed.

> Dear Lord,
> Thank you that I may come to you when I'm oppressed. You are a refuge for me in times of trouble. I know your mercy and I count on you for help. You will never forsake my trust in you. (See Ps. 9:9–10.)
> Thank you that I can trade my troubled heart for your peace. I trust in you and your Son. (See John 14:1–2.)
> Thank you that I do not have to worry about anything, but with this prayer and thanksgiving, I can tell you about my need of _____ and know that you have heard and answered me. Thank you for the peace that comes when I surrender my needs to you and trust in Christ Jesus. (See Phil. 4:5–7.)

I continue to cast all my worries and cares on you because you always think about me and watch over everything that concerns me. (See 1 Peter 5:7.)

In Jesus' blessed name,

Amen.

6

What to Pray
When You've Been Betrayed

Opposition is not only evidence that God is blessing, but it is also an opportunity for us to grow. . . . "God had one Son without sin," said Charles Spurgeon, "but he never had a son without a trial."

—Warren W. Wiersbe

A couple of years ago I was in downtown Hilo, Hawaii, when I discovered a bookstore with a lovely display of a book called *Da Jesus Book*. Curious, I picked up a copy to see what it was. To my delight, I discovered a Wycliffe translation of the New Testament in the Hawaiian pidgin language.

Hawaiian pidgin is a mix of several languages including English, Japanese, French, Chinese, and Polynesian. It's still spoken on the Islands—about half of the Hawaiian people speak pidgin before they learn to speak English. The wonderful thing about this Hawaiian pidgin translation of the

Bible is it's "English" enough that even I can understand it. (And so can you.)

For example, here's the NIV translation of Mark 11:25, which states: "And when you stand praying, if you hold anything against anyone, forgive him, so that your Father in heaven may forgive you your sins."

The same passage in *Da Jesus Book* says: "Every time you guys stand up an pray, if you huhu wit somebody, you gotta let dem go, an no feel huhu wit dem. If you do dat, den yoa Fadda dat stay inside da sky, he goin let you guys go, an no feel huhu bout da bad kine stuff you guys wen do."[1]

Huhu, huh? I get it. We have to let go of our huhus (anger) because God has had plenty of opportunity to hold huhus against us. He lets go of his huhus against us, and we should let go of our huhus against others. That sounds like more than a fair trade.

> We have to let go of our huhus (anger) because God has had plenty of opportunity to hold huhus against us. He lets go of his huhus against us, and we should let go of our huhus against others. That sounds like more than a fair trade.

Clear? Yeah, except for one thing. Some huhus are no laughing matter. As you'll read in the following letter to me from Betrayed.

Dear Linda,

Until a few days ago my life was a good one.

That is, until my best friend went behind my back and lied to my boss about me. Not only did she get my promotion, my employer accused me of stealing. I was devastated.

Still, I felt safe in my marriage. But that night, I picked up the phone and caught my husband talking to his girlfriend. I was shocked.

Later, when he admitted to the affair, he told me he's never loved me. He packed his bags and walked out. That was three days ago.

My very world has been rocked. I hate my husband, I hate my friend, and now I hate myself.

—Betrayed

My response:

Dear Betrayed,

What both your husband and friend did to you was wrong. They both betrayed you. But you do not deserve the effects of the resulting hate and anger that is overwhelming you. Hate can kill you; bitterness will imprison you. Both can destroy your life—not your friend's or your husband's life.

What can you do to be free? It may take some time, but you need to give God the hate and anger you feel and ask him to help you let go of it. You also need to forgive. Not because your husband or friend deserve it, but because you deserve to get on with your life.

Would you be willing to pray this prayer? *Lord, in Jesus' name, I give you the hate and anger I feel. Lord, give me the strength to let go of my bitterness.*

Okay, this is good, but there's one more prayer to go. It may feel costly, though it will give you your freedom. *Lord, give me the strength to forgive this offense. All this I pray in Jesus' name.*

You may need to pray these prayers every time the anger rises up in you.

You are not justifying the wrong committed against you. You are simply becoming free from the bondage of emotions like hatred, anger, and bitterness.

Quit thinking so much about the offenses. Instead, think about God's great love for you. Did you know that when your husband and so-called friend betrayed you, it was as if the betrayal was committed against Jesus himself? Unless they become reconciled with God, they could be in big trouble.

If you can break free of your bitterness through God's strength, you will be free to get on with your life.

The journey will probably not happen overnight, but you will get there, one step at a time. You will know you have arrived when you can ask God to help the ones who wronged you. Keep praying and you will achieve your goal.

Your friend,

Linda

Betrayed has a big task ahead of her. Forgiveness is often difficult to achieve. But with God's help, it's possible. Please don't think I don't know what I'm talking about. I do. It's sometimes very hard to practice what you preach. I know this all too well.

"Linda," my mother's voice crackled across the phone line, "Sharon Cain disappeared last weekend!"

I felt a sudden sickness in the pit of my stomach. "You're kidding! I saw Sharon Saturday. What happened?"

My mother paused. "That's the day she was reported missing. Apparently, she and her husband were walking home from the Gateway Shopping Center after their car broke down."

I sat down, overwhelmed. "That's where I saw her," I stammered. "I waved at her, but she didn't see me. It . . . it never occurred to me she needed help. I thought she and her husband were heading for a nearby restaurant!"

My mother continued to update me as news reports drifted in. Shortly after passing me, Sharon's husband had sprinted ahead, planning to return for his wife with their other car.

> You are not justifying the wrong committed against you. You are simply becoming free from the bondage of emotions like hatred, anger, and bitterness.

Meanwhile, a stranger accelerated down the road toward Sharon. When he saw her walking alone, he screeched to a halt, swung open the car door, and yanked her inside by her hair. Then he drove to an isolated beach on the Texas Gulf Coast. After brutalizing her, he abandoned her, leaving her to die, buried alive in the sand.

Over the next few days, the ugly facts played over and over in my mind. The more I thought about them, the more furious I became with myself for not getting the couple's attention. God had put them directly in my path and I'd blown it. *I didn't know!* I argued with my conscience. I couldn't have known Sharon was in danger. In a sense, I was also a victim of this senseless tragedy.

I spent the next few nights in sleeplessness, turning the blame and anger from myself to Sharon's murderer. Months later, when Thomas Wilson was tried and sentenced to die by electrocution, I was elated. I believed even hell was too good for this man. Over time, my bitterness only intensified.

Then one Sunday morning, I listened to our pastor speak from Mark 11:25: "And when you stand praying, if you hold anything against anyone, forgive him, so that your Father in heaven may forgive you your sins."

This message shocked me. This couldn't possibly apply to me and my hatred for Sharon's killer, could it? But I already knew that it did.

It isn't fair, I silently screamed. *That man had no right to rob Sharon of her life! I can't believe you would want me to forgive him after what he did!*

I wrestled silently for months, contemplating the monstrous wrong committed against Sharon, her family, and her friends. I even mourned for the children she would never bear. Thomas Wilson's actions were unjustifiable, and therefore, I concluded, unforgivable.

As I sat on my sofa one evening, a question came to mind: to receive God's forgiveness, must one's sin always be accompanied by a good excuse? I flipped through my Bible to Romans 3:23–24: "For all have sinned and fall short of the glory of God, and are justified freely by his grace through the redemption that came by Christ Jesus."

According to that passage, God's forgiveness is given freely, no matter the circumstances.

> According to that passage, God's forgiveness is given freely, no matter the circumstances.

In one painful moment, I knew I had to forgive Thomas Wilson—regardless of his crime—excuse or no excuse. My heart rebelled as my mind made a decision. It would be hard to give up my hatred, like exchanging a custom-fitted garment for one much too big. Even so, I weakly told the Lord that with his help, I was willing to try to forgive this man, though it seemed far beyond my ability.

My first problem was how. How do I go about forgiving the unforgivable? And how would I know if I'd succeeded? Though several years had passed, the mere mention of Thomas Wilson's name still sent shivers down my spine.

While reading one day, I saw an item about an organization called Death Row Support Project. I began to feel the Lord prompting me to test my so-called forgiveness on a real person.

"Don't do it, Linda," my mother cautioned. "Think of the victims' families."

"I sympathize with them," I agreed. "But I have to find out how big God's forgiveness really is."

After much trepidation and a few crumpled starts, I wrote asking the project to send me the name of a death-row inmate with whom I could correspond. I secretly hoped I would get the name of someone whose crime would be easy to forgive.

When the letter arrived from the project, I opened it with trembling hands. I was shocked to read the group had sent me the name of Johnny Lee Simpson, a convicted murderer from my own hometown of Beaumont, Texas.

My mother was horrified. "He killed two women during a bank robbery! First he shared a cup of coffee with them, then he shot each of them in the head!"

Pregnant with my first child, I, too, was appalled this man had killed two young mothers. With difficulty, I began writing to Johnny. And the sensitive replies that came from this intelligent, fifty-year-old convict amazed me.

"Who would have thought my life would have turned out like this?" Johnny wrote. "There was a time when I taught a boys' Sunday school class. But I've turned my back on all that. Don't pity me. I've made my own choices. I want to die and go to hell to pay the debt I owe society."

"But Johnny, Jesus has already done that for you," I wrote back, desperate for him to understand. He didn't.

Through our correspondence, Johnny shared in my joy over the birth of my daughter, Laura, and grieved with me when she was injured in that terrible car crash. He wrote, "I sat up all night in my cell and thought solely of Laura and you in that hospital. Before daylight, I got the definite feeling that Laura was going to be fine and would grow into a lovely woman. You are not alone."

Somehow, it was easier for me to forgive Johnny, not because he deserved it, but because God's hand was moving in our lives. I could feel God's love and compassion for him, just as he'd felt God's love and compassion for us.

One March morning, Johnny sent bad news: "An hour ago, I received another date of execution for May the 3rd. As I have turned my back on my own faith, I shall not be a hypocrite and ask for God's forgiveness. Please understand."

"But Johnny," I wrote in my next letter, "none of us deserves God's forgiveness. Can't you see that God will look past your sins, if you only ask?"

His letter was a blow: "Many long and lost years ago I'd a deep and abiding faith, which I alone destroyed. In so doing, I destroyed myself. I cannot look back. I will die without God."

With Johnny's execution date weeks away, I yearned to see him experience God's redeeming power. As I sat at my computer keyboard, trying to define God's forgiveness for Johnny in a letter, the enormity of his grace and mercy became real to me. With great anticipation and prayer, I mailed my letter and waited for a response. But as it turned out, God proved himself to Johnny without my help.

"I understand now. Jesus has forgiven even me, even though I don't deserve it. I'm in his kingdom now."

"Very late Thursday night," Johnny wrote, "I had my back turned to the bars . . . listening to all the yelling and cussing, but suddenly, I did not hear a sound, only a voice within me saying, 'You shall not die, there are things you have to do.'

"Later, my Bible dropped from the shelf onto my bunk. I picked it up and it fell open to Colossians 1:13–14: 'For he has rescued us from the dominion of darkness and brought us into the kingdom of the Son he loves, in whom we have redemption, the forgiveness of sins.' I understand now. Jesus has forgiven even me, even though I don't deserve it. I'm in his kingdom now."

I read the letter with joy, realizing that in the process of becoming Johnny's friend, the Lord totally removed the last traces of bitterness from my spirit over the murder of my friend Sharon. I was wonderfully free!

And Johnny? After a year of leading a Bible study in his cellblock and writing letters to children in a hospital cancer ward, he faced his final execution date. He's with his Creator now, a forgiven man. Someday, when I cross over to heaven, I will give Johnny a great big hug. I may even say, "I told you so."

Eyewitnessing Freedom

While speaking to a women's church group from San Diego, I asked my audience a hypothetical question: "Is there ever an instance when we shouldn't forgive another?"

Much to my surprise, a lady in the audience answered as if we were sitting across from one another chatting over a cup of tea. "I can't forgive something that happened to me. The person who hurt me is dead, and I hope he's where he belongs."

I said, "What that man did to you was wrong. But think about it. Do you deserve to let that man come between you and your relationship with God? Do you realize that's what you are doing?"

"I never thought about it that way," she admitted.

"This man has hurt you enough," I said. "Give God your bitterness. Are you willing?"

"I don't know," she said.

"Are you willing to be willing?" I asked.

"Yes," she said.

I looked around the group. "Who is willing to pray for Rhonda?" I asked.

The whole room stood to their feet, and her friends gathered around her. One began, "Sweetie, we'll pray for you. It's time you got set free." And pray her friends did. Finally, I said, "Rhonda, are you ready to let go?"

"Yes," she said with tears streaming down her cheeks.

I led her in a simple prayer. "Dear Lord, as an act of my will, through your power, I release the man who wronged me. I forgive him with and through your power. In Jesus' name, amen."

After the prayer, her friends cheered and she rose from her chair. "I'm free of him. I'm free!" she shouted.

At another speaking engagement in New Jersey, I led the group through several prayers of releasing burdens and requesting forgiveness. At the close of the meeting, we began to sing praise songs, when God's sweet presence entered the room. Women sank to their knees, and soft weeping filled the room. It was one of the most incredible times of refreshing I've ever seen.

A woman approached me. "Could you come and talk to my friend Nina?" she asked.

When I found Nina, a beautiful young Hispanic woman, she told me in broken English, "I speak Spanish, and I could not understand enough of what you said to get set free like the others. I want to be free too."

"Nina, what's happened? What's troubling you?"

Tears sprang forth. Through an interpreter, she said, "It's my daughter. She's only nine years old. I've discovered our neighbor, a man I trusted, has been molesting her for years." Nina sank to her knees and pounded the seat of her chair as she wept, "Why, why, why did this have to happen to my little girl?"

I wrapped my arms around her. "Nina, what that man did to your little girl was wrong. He shouldn't have done that. But that doesn't mean God can't meet your daughter where she is. That doesn't mean God has forgotten your daughter."

"But it hurts so bad."

"Yes. But God has a plan for you and for your daughter. You have to give him this situation."

Nina's sobbing stopped. "I'm ready." She prayed, "Lord, I'm so heartbroken about what my neighbor did to my daughter. It was wrong. It shouldn't have happened. But I know I can give this situation to you. I know that you can take a bad situation and turn it into good. I give you my daughter's precious life, and by an act of my will, and through your power, I ask you to help me forgive this man for what he's done."

She looked up at me, peace shining in her tearstained eyes. She smiled, emotionally spent but filled with joy. "I'm free," she said. "I'm free. God has set me free. I now know my daughter has a future and a hope."

Yes, Nina. In God, she certainly does.

What about You?

One of the leaders of the New Jersey event asked me, "What happened here tonight? What did you do?"

"I didn't do anything," I said. "But when we began to praise the Lord, the Spirit of God fell and set his daughters free."

God is not a respecter of denominational lines. I've seen him move like this in all camps. And I know when the Spirit moves, no one is left unchanged, including me.

What about you? Do you have anger and bitterness in your heart? Please, offer it as a sacrificial offering to the Lord. I'm not saying that we can ever justify the wrongs that have been committed against you. But I do know that holding on to your bitterness and anger will not make you feel better.

Besides, you were not designed to be a vessel to hold that kind of pain. God wants to take all your hurt and bitterness. Are you ready to give it to him? Are you ready to let go?

Pray the following:

Dear Lord,
    You know about my betrayal. You know about my anger and bitterness toward _____.
    I am too weak to forgive in this situation, so I give it to you. Please forgive for me, through your power. I lay my emotions at your feet.
    In Jesus' name,
    Amen.

What to Do Next

Don't retaliate against the one who wronged you. That's not your responsibility. Because you've given this situation to God, that's his business, not yours.

Pray for the One(s) Who Wronged You

This is a sure mark of spiritual growth on your part. Leonard Ravenhill, one of the greatest twentieth-century authorities on revival, said, "Notice, we never pray for folks we gossip about, and we never gossip about the folk for whom we pray! For prayer is a great deterrent."[2]

Great observation, which leads me to say, next time you are tempted to talk about the one who wronged you, try praying instead.

Apologize for Others

In 1 Samuel 25, we read about an incident we don't hear about from the pulpit very often. It's the story of Abigail, a woman who apologized on behalf of her stupid husband. You see, David requested payment for protecting Nabal's flock from looters. But instead of sending a thank-you note with a check inside, Nabal sent David an insult. David was so furious over this lack of gratitude and respect, he vowed to kill Nabal and all the men of his household.

When Nabal's wife heard of her husband's stupidity, she didn't wait to argue; instead, she hurried to David herself. David and his men were already on their way to seek revenge when Abigail fell at his feet, offering David gifts and apologizing for her husband's rude behavior.

Abigail's wisdom and heroic action prevented a slaughter. After the sudden death of her foolish husband (he died of a heart attack upon learning David was on his way to kill him), Abigail became David's wife.

There's a time to apologize on behalf of those who may not even be able to see the error of their ways. This kind of intervention can go a long way toward preventing further tragedy. As the Word says, "Blessed are the peacemakers" (Matt. 5:9).

Apologize for Yourself

I once had a manager who time and again set me up for failure. When I got tired of trying to defend myself, I finally told him what I really thought. The memory of the words I'd spoken in anger haunted me even after I changed jobs. Finally, I asked the Lord to provide an opportunity for me to apologize to this man.

An opportunity presented itself years later when I found myself standing behind my former boss and his wife in a line at the grocery store. I knew God had provided this time and place, and I was determined to take advantage of it. I said to the man who had once so greatly offended me, "I'm glad I ran into you and your wife tonight. I've always felt badly about the way I spoke to you, and I'd like to apologize to you for the things I said."

My former manager smiled. "It's okay," he said. "I apologize too."

His wife smiled. "That was a bad time, but we've all moved on."

I left the grocery store that night feeling ten pounds lighter. That tiny conversation was so freeing to all of us.

Even though I was willing to apologize sooner, God was in charge of the timing. And his timing is perfect. I don't know why God waited until that particular moment, but I do know my former manager accepted my apology, and his apology was accepted by me. God is good.

Create Opportunities for Reconciliation

Many years ago, someone in the publishing industry betrayed me. In the years that passed, I longed for reconciliation, but I felt I'd done nothing for which to apologize, so I wasn't sure how to proceed.

Then the day came this man and I were on staff at the same writers' conference. There I approached him and said, "I was wondering if we could put the past behind us and be friends."

He smiled and said, "Linda, of course."

I extended my hand and said, "Then, can we shake on it?"

We did, and with that, I felt the wall between us crumble. Now, when I see this gentleman, I know he's not my enemy but my brother in the Lord.

No, I didn't apologize, and come to think of it, neither did he. However, we were able to acknowledge our differences and move on.

Praying Scripture

Pray these paraphrased verses:

Dear Lord,

I love my loved ones, of course; but help me to love my enemies and pray for those who persecute me. (See Matt. 5:43–45.)

Help me to be slow to anger and also to overlook an offense. (See Prov. 19:11.)

If my enemy is hungry or needy, give me an opportunity to feed and provide for him. Thank you for the blessing that comes from such actions. (See Prov. 25:21–22.)

As I pray, bring to mind those I need to forgive and help me do so, so that you may also forgive me. (See Mark 11:25.)

In Jesus' name,

Amen.

7

What to Pray
When Everything Goes Wrong

To a great extent we find that we must sow in tears before we
can reap in joy. . . . You may expect a blessing in serving God if
you are enabled to persevere under many discouragements.

—Charles Spurgeon

Have you ever had a really bad day?

A few years ago I started a trip to San Antonio, Texas, by
praying for "traveling mercies."

The first leg of my flight landed me in Dallas, Texas, where
I had to change planes. As soon as I was buckled into my San
Antonio flight I closed my eyes and napped through take-
off. But twenty minutes into the flight my pounding heart
jarred me out of my rest. I opened my eyes and saw what
appeared to be smoke curling out of the air vents. I turned
to my neighbor, whose eyes were as wide as mine. "Is that
smoke?" I asked.

He nodded mutely as if in shock.

The voice of the captain blared on the overhead speakers, "This is an emergency. Our jet is on fire. I've radioed Dallas and we are returning to the airport. We'll be landing shortly. Good luck, everyone."

The captain rolled the jet into a tight U-turn, and the plane shook violently as we barreled back to Dallas. I looked around at the passengers. They sat rigid in their seats, their eyes wide. Unlike the movie *Airplane*, no one pulled out their guitar to sing "Kumbaya," including me.

I had once co-written a book called *Share Jesus Without Fear*. Why didn't I seem to be able to take the moment and do just that with the wide-eyed man next to me? Instead, I stared out the window and prayed for mercy. I could see Grapevine, Texas, directly below us. We were so close to the ground I could read the names of the churches we flew over. Moments later, the airport lined with emergency vehicles was within sight. When the wheels tipped to touch the runway we held our breath, hoping the plane wouldn't break apart or burst into flames.

Neither happened.

But we were too shocked to cheer so we sat in silence as the plane taxied directly to the gate where the flight attendants unlocked the doors into the jetway.

The passengers rose as one and we each walked past the captain as we exited the plane. With tears in his eyes, he bid each of us good-bye with a warm handshake. It was as if he was quietly saying to each of us, "I saved you, and you, and you . . ."

I stepped into the terminal—never happier to see an airport. I was greeted by an airline employee who handed me a five-dollar phone card and a seven-dollar food voucher, the apparent sum value of my life.

Later that evening I boarded another plane before finally making it to my hotel in San Antonio. Once in my room,

I flipped on the TV and watched as Ted Koppel said, "An airliner made an emergency landing today in Dallas when the air conditioning system caught fire."

I said as if to Ted, "Oh yeah, I remember that."

That night, the opening session and speakers at the convention were marvelous. Afterwards, I decided I would go to the prayer meeting that always met the first night of the convention. I wasn't sure how to get there until I found an acquaintance who said, "That's where I'm headed, follow me."

We rushed to the open door of the elevator and stared into the silver cavity before us. It was jammed with people—in fact, the entire speakers' association board of directors stood in the back with another layer of people smashed in front of them. I turned to my friend and said, "I guess we'll have to wait for the next elevator."

But instead of waiting with me, this gentleman pushed his way inside, turned around, and stared back at me.

As he was the one who knew the way to the prayer meeting, I had to make a split decision. So being a mature believer, I, too, pushed my way inside as the elevator door slid shut. Our sardine can traveled up about thirty-two floors before it came to an unexpected halt. At first no one breathed as the ugly truth sunk in. We were stuck!

I was filled with embarrassment as I imagined what everyone was thinking. "Lady, if you hadn't elbowed your way inside, this wouldn't have happened and we wouldn't be over the weight limit."

We were packed so tight it was almost impossible to locate the emergency phone or even reach our cell phones. The woman who managed to accomplish this feat told us, "They're coming to get us out."

That's when I noticed everyone had the same deer-in-the-headlights expression I'd seen on the burning jet. The extra-large man in the back of the elevator noticed it too and tried to break the tension. As he loomed over us he said, "Pardon me, but I have gas." No one laughed, but I think the woman next to me may have fainted. It was hard to tell because our bodies held her in place.

Soon workmen forced hooks between the door of the elevator and pried it open. But now we had a new obstacle. We'd halted between floors and now had to scale six feet to freedom. Guess who was at the front of the line? Me!

I was wearing a long, elastic-waist broomstick skirt. The kind that can easily pull off your hips when you are scaling walls. Guess what I wasn't wearing? My slip. Yep, I'd accidentally left it at home. So, there I was, with the entire NSA board behind me, trying to scale a wall in an elastic skirt with no slip.

I tried to climb out without climbing out of my skirt. But my attempts were getting me nowhere. I'd managed to pull myself near the top, but I didn't have enough strength to climb out when suddenly, that big guy in the rear of the elevator grabbed me and threw me out the elevator door. As I slid across the carpet on my stomach, I was relieved to realize my hips were too big for that skirt to ever slide off!

So I guess you could say I had a really terrible, no good, very bad day.

Or had I?

I'd survived a would-be fiery plane crash and a stuck elevator *and* kept my skirt on. God had answered my morning prayer. He had granted me mercy.

But you have to wonder, what's the point of all the crazi-

> I'd survived a would-be fiery plane crash and a stuck elevator *and* kept my skirt on. God had answered my morning prayer. He had granted me mercy.

ness? Where's God in these details? Why did he allow these things to happen in the first place?

Great questions, the kinds of questions you may have asked God yourself. Even Job asked the "why" question. But did you know that God never answered him? Instead, God asked Job, "So, where were you when I created the world?"

In other words, God answered by saying, "Who are you to question me?"

Yikes! God has an excellent point. We are not God. We do not know his mind, his purposes, or his ways to accomplish them.

For all I know, God allows things to happen—things like me gliding through the skies in a burning airplane, getting stuck in an elevator, my daughter spending a year in a coma—to accomplish a purpose I couldn't begin to imagine.

It's a lot like a woman I met back East. She took me aside during a break at the conference where I was speaking.

"I want to tell you a story," she said. "It's about my brother, a New York City fireman who died a very terrible death to cancer. We fought the good fight of faith and prayed for his healing. But he died anyway. It was so hard to understand why God would take this wonderful young man.

"That is, until 9/11. You see, my brother's co-workers were among the firemen at the World Trade Center and most of them died in the rubble. Later the chaplain told me, 'Now we finally understand why God took your brother. For his squad witnessed how your brother got ready to meet the Lord. Your brother helped prepare them for their own deaths. And you can be sure your brother was standing on the other side, greeting his brothers as they entered into the presence of God.'"

Wow, how's that for changing one's perspective of a tragic death?

So though we may not be able to figure out all the reasons why bad things happen, we can know who to trust through whatever difficult circumstances come our way—our Lord himself.

I've changed the way I pray before a trip. Oh yes, I still pray for traveling mercies. One definition of mercy on Dictionary.com is "something for which to be thankful." I'm thankful for my Dallas/San Antonio trip. It was a mercy I got out alive.

But sometimes, I want more than mercy, I want grace.

Dictionary.com says of grace, "the free and unmerited favor or beneficence of God." Mercy is wonderful, but grace is sweeter.

> But sometimes, I want more than mercy, I want grace.

Since I have been praying for traveling mercies and grace, thankfully I've not had to endure any more burning planes or stuck elevators.

Recently, an online Christian author's loop discussed what to do about "the fear of flying," which plagues several of our members.

We concluded that the traveler must always be prepared to meet their maker even before getting on the plane. One author suggested we pray, "God, my life belongs to you. You can take it now or take it later. It's up to you."

That's a prayer we should be ready to pray no matter if we're in the skies, driving through traffic, on the job, or even at home. In fact, we should trust God enough to give him our lives, daily.

Try this as a morning prayer:

Dear Lord,
Today, I give you my day and my life. Please guide my feet in your purposes. And Lord, make my path straight. Cover it with your mercy and grace.
In Jesus' name,
Amen.

This is a great prayer, and one I pray daily. I believe God answers this prayer by helping me to live my life on purpose—his purpose. Proverbs 3:5–6 says: "Trust in the LORD with all your heart and lean not on your own understanding; in all your ways acknowledge him, and he will make your paths straight."

But as much as mercy and grace abounds, each one of us will discover struggles and trials along the way. These struggles and trials will make us stronger and present opportunities to expand our prayer life. For example, when we are going through a difficult time, we should:

- Seek God
- Pray specifically
- Trust God

Seek God

Not long ago, I got an email from a man who said, "Life stinks. Everything always goes wrong."

I wrote back, "You're right, of course. Sometimes life ain't so grand. But here's a quote from Jesus that might help, from James 5:13, which says, 'Is any one of you in trouble? He should pray.'"

We should pray! What a concept. So the answer to the question of how to pray in times of trouble is an interesting one. We turn to God, give him the trouble to carry, and trust him with the result.

For example, if you were facing a great trouble, you might pray:

Dear Lord,
Help! I'm in trouble. You asked me to cast my burdens on you, so I give you this trouble. Show me what you would

have me do. Give me clear direction. Help me to wait on you as I trust you with the result. I know that all things work together for the good of those who love you. I love you and I know that you love me too. I know I can trust you, and for that, I thank you. I thank you for turning this situation into a miracle.

In Jesus' name,
Amen.

Pray Specifically

Charles Haddon Spurgeon, one of England's best known and most loved preachers for most of the second half of the nineteenth century, once said, "There is a general kind of praying which fails for lack of precision. It is as if a regiment of soldiers should all fire off their guns anywhere. Possibly somebody would be killed, but the majority of the enemy would be missed."[1]

Spurgeon is making a great point: there are times we need to pray with precision. "Lord, if it be your will, please help me find a job that would utilize my skills and talents and allow me to better provide for my family" may serve as a better prayer in a time of unemployment than a prayer like, "Lord, bless me."

Not that the "bless me" prayer is inappropriate, but its lack of precision may keep you from missing the joy of seeing God answer your more specific prayer specifically.

Trust God

This is the area where we fail the most. Our perspective is not a heavenly one, so we can sometimes only imagine one acceptable answer to a prayer request. But I have to ask, what would happen if we trusted God to answer his own way instead of our way? Are you willing to take that risk?

If you revisit my example of the prayer request for a job, notice it was prefaced with, "Lord, if it be your will."

This phrase is simply a way to acknowledge that you are trusting God to answer your needs his way.

Recently, I interviewed a couple who had lost their twenty-three-year-old daughter, a beautiful girl who had been struck by lightning on a golf course. The girl had lived for three years in a sort of twilight, able to understand but not able to talk or care for herself. As her death was still recent, I wasn't sure why this couple wanted to come on the TV program. I asked them about it before the show. "What is it you want to say to our audience?"

When they couldn't give me what I felt was a satisfactory answer, I got nervous. Had they simply come to publically vent their heartache?

It wasn't until we got in front of the cameras that I "got" their message. The father said, "How many of us have had God say 'no' to a prayer request and not realized it was for our own good? That's what happened to us. Two and a half years after our daughter was struck by lightning, her mother and I begged God to send us a night nurse, a caregiver who would sit with Rachel at night so that we could get some needed rest. But our prayers went unanswered for six months. That meant my wife and I had to take turns taking care of our daughter at night by ourselves.

"I always took the first shift. I spent it reading Scripture to my daughter, praying with her and talking with her about her life and God. It was a precious time. But little did I know Rachel was living her last days on earth. One night, only minutes after I kissed her good night, her mother discovered she was gone. She had suddenly slipped away to be with the Lord."

With tears rolling down his cheeks, this dear father said, "Now when I look back, how I thank God that he didn't answer my prayers for a night nurse, because if he had, I would have missed that precious time I had with Rachel. God not answering my prayer was one of the greatest gifts he's ever given me."

Now that's a powerful message. It illustrates we can trust God even when he says no.

Praying Scripture

Here is a Scripture prayer I recommend you pray when everything goes wrong:

> Dear Lord,
> I trust in you and acknowledge that you have everything under control and you are making my paths straight. (See Prov. 3:5–6.)
> I delight in your ways, Lord, so I ask you to make my path firm. I know that even if I stumble, I will not fall, for you have taken hold of my hand. (See Ps. 37:23–24.)
> I will seek you, O Lord, and you will give me success. (See 2 Chron. 26:5.)
> You have plans for me, to prosper me and not to harm me, to give me hope and a future. I will call upon you and you will hear me. I will find you when I seek you with my whole heart. (See Jer. 29:11–14.)

Below is another portion of Scripture I could not resist paraphrasing into a prayer: Psalm 27.

> Dear Lord,
> There is no one to fear when I am standing in your light. For you are my salvation and my strength. When evil men

try to attack, they shall trip and fall. Even if an army comes to wage war against me (or a hurricane, tornado, or tsunami roar toward my town), I will not be afraid, for I am confident in you.

I seek your face and know that I will spend eternity with you. There, I will forever see your beauty.

Today, tomorrow, if trouble should come, you will keep me safe. You will hide me. In the end, I will be the victor, shouting for joy. I will sing praises to the Lord most high.

Lord, hear me when I call. Answer me and show me your mercy. My heart longs to seek your face. Do not hide from me or turn away in anger. You have been my helper, so please do not reject or forsake me, God my Savior. Even if my mother and father turn me away, you, oh Lord, will welcome me. Teach me your way, oh Lord, and make my path straight. Deliver me from my enemies.

I know I will see the answer to my prayers in this lifetime. Therefore, Lord, I wait for you. The thought of you gives me strength and helps me to take heart.

In Jesus' name,

Amen.

8

What to Pray in Difficult Financial Situations

I have held many things in my hands, and I have lost them all; but whatever I have placed in God's hands, that I still possess.

—Martin Luther

Money is such an important topic that some readers (perhaps even you) have skipped ahead to this chapter, hoping to pray a miraculous prayer to help resolve financial troubles.

Yes, you will find some great prayers here, but before you skip ahead, please take a few moments to learn how to prepare your heart for such prayers. Because honestly, God looks at your heart when you send him your financial request.

It's true that God owns the cattle on a thousand hills, not to mention all the gold in the ocean as well as the gems in the hearts of the mountains. So what would it hurt him to share some of his lavish riches with you? You may even ask, *Why doesn't God provide for me the way I think he should?*

First, consider this: our values and God's values are not always one and the same. But they could be. The more we can see things from God's perspective, the more his treasures will become what we treasure.

Otherwise, we might experience the disappointment of the man who spent a lifetime praying God would allow him to take his earthly treasure into heaven. God finally agreed: "Okay, you get to pack one suitcase with whatever you want."

The man bought the largest rolling suitcase he could find. He spent the rest of his life packing it with gold dust, gold bars, gold nuggets, and gold coins of all shapes and varieties. Finally the day arrived when he entered into glory, and he tugged his heavy load to the pearly gates.

> The more we can see things from God's perspective, the more his treasures will become what we treasure.

Saint Peter tried to stop him. He said, "Sir, you're not allowed to bring anything into heaven."

The man produced a document signed by God himself. "It's okay, Pete. I got a waiver."

Peter scratched his bearded chin as he read the paper. "Well, everything's in order. So, what did you decide to bring with you?"

Proudly, the man unzipped his suitcase, and Peter gasped at the glitter of gold that spilled forth at his feet.

"Impressive, huh?" the man said proudly as he stood next to his treasure.

"Not really, sir," Saint Peter remarked. "Why would you bring a suitcase full of pavement?"

I hope I don't try to drag something as worthless as gold through the gates of heaven, though I do hope to bring treasures of eternal value—my family and friends.

That's a lovely sentiment, you might say, but I'm not in heaven yet. I'm still here on this earth, and my mortgage bill is sitting in my mailbox along with a couple of credit card bills. Not only that, but (gasp), my gas tank is empty. Not to mention that I'm out of eggs and milk. Heavenly treasure may be my ultimate goal, but in the meantime, I've got to send Uncle Sam, my dentist, not to mention the utility company, a check or two. As far as I know, these earthly bill collectors don't accept "heavenly" treasury bills.

True enough. Bills must be paid, provisions must be purchased, and you don't have access to your heavenly bank account yet. Or, do you?

After all, Philippians 4:19 says, "And my God will meet all your needs according to his glorious riches in Christ Jesus."

How does one live this Scripture?

Let's look deeper. Did you know this declaration was originally written to the saints at Philippi? These were the very men and women who supported Paul financially. In fact, Paul wrote this proclamation just after thanking them for their support. (See vv. 14–18.)

So, in other words, Paul was writing obedient believers who were giving to God's work. He was telling them that because they supported God's work by providing for his (Paul's) needs, God would provide for their needs.

> I hope I don't try to drag something as worthless as gold through the gates of heaven, though I do hope to bring treasures of eternal value—my family and friends.

To me, this says that our obedience to God in financial matters is a good indication of God's continued provision. Do you feel you are honoring God with your giving? If not, what should you do differently? These are good questions we'll soon discuss. (As I'm not passing an offering plate at the end of this chapter, you don't need to worry that I'm trying to get into your pocket book. I'm trying to show you the truth.)

For now, let's look at a couple of Scriptures found in this same chapter. A few verses earlier we read, "Do not be anxious about anything, but in everything, by prayer and petition, with thanksgiving, present your requests to God. And the peace of God, which transcends all understanding, will guard your hearts and your minds in Christ Jesus" (vv. 6–7).

At this point in this chapter, Paul was writing about peace. He's telling his readers to avoid worry by giving their requests to God with prayer and thanksgiving.

This is such encouragement. God hears our requests and responds with peace. That peace may come in one of two ways—as a spiritual gift from God and/or as an understanding that we can trust God as our provider.

In fact, one of God's many names is Jehovah Jireh, which means "God is our provider." This is the name Abraham gave to God on Mount Moriah, when God provided a sacrificial goat to be used as a burnt offering in place of Abraham's own son.

> Debt-free living is about getting ourselves right spiritually and emotionally so we can use our financial tools in a God-directed way.

Therefore we can rejoice that God provides. However, just because you've laid out your financial problems in prayer doesn't mean you're free from responsible behavior. Author and speaker Karen O'Connor has said that true recovery from financial difficulties comes when we entrust our lives and our situations to God.

She says, "Debt-free living is about getting ourselves right spiritually and emotionally so we can use our financial tools in a God-directed way."

Karen explains that many hurting people have no idea how spiritually bankrupt they are. She knows because in her words, "I was one of them. I could not even imagine a life without financial struggle. But the very moment I told God I was willing to recover from self-destructive behavior, things began to miraculously change."

She gave God her debts and spending behavior. She says, "He closed the old account and opened a new one in partnership with me—a spiritual bank account that deals in the currency of surrender, simplicity, solvency, and serenity—which he provided when I, powerless and despondent, turned to him."

Karen explains surrender, simplicity, solvency, and serenity like this:

Surrender. "I discovered that no lasting change could occur or continue without giving complete control over to the Lord. After I began releasing my fears and failings to him each morning in prayer, I was in a position to consider simplifying my life instead of giving in to the pressure of society to acquire and accumulate."

Simplicity. "Debt-free living is simple living! I stopped using credit cards. I stopped buying what we couldn't afford and didn't need. It required daily vigilance only possible with God at my side."

Solvency. "Solvency—the ability to pay all that one owes—is the goal of anyone who desires real freedom. But there remained for me a great gap between the desire and the reality. That is when Twelve-Step programs such as Debtors Anonymous and other support groups became my lifeline. In these meetings, I was able to share my victories and my defeats and be heard, understood, and loved."

Serenity. "Serenity is a spiritual discipline that brings about a state of total well-being as we come to rest in God. It is where I live today. As I continue the spiritual journey of living a debt-free life, I turn daily to these disciplines, like streams in the desert, to refresh my spirit when I feel dry, and to guide me when I feel lost. No longer do I live in fear, for 'the Lord God is a sun and shield . . . no good thing will he withhold from those who walk uprightly' (Ps. 84:11)."[1]

To summarize her financial prayer and life plan, Karen says,

> Simplicity provides a solid foundation on which solvency can be practiced. When I made a sincere commitment to remain solvent, I was then in a position to give to the church and to charities. For the past ten years I have not missed putting a check in the offering plate.
>
> Practicing solvency also brought me to a place of willingness to learn all I could about financial matters. This included taking an interest in managing my checking accounts, handling cash in responsible ways, planning for my future, and setting aside money for emergencies, investments, vacations, and retirement.
>
> It included praying for guidance about who to talk with, which seminars to attend, what books to read. The discipline of solvency was for me the outworking of an inward commitment to become a good steward of the resources God provided and it paved the way for a life of serenity.

I want to thank Karen for allowing me to share her story. Her message illustrates that God does not provide a divine piggy bank for us to dip into at every whim. God expects us to be responsible stewards of his provisions.

I have discovered, however, God loves to provide for us. I remember a day when Laura was in the hospital, still in a coma. Our insurance was in question because of a technicality, and I was scared to death. I correctly guessed it would take a million dollars to get Laura out of the hospital, and needless to say, we didn't have a million dollars.

But I didn't panic. As I stood at the end of Laura's hospital bed one afternoon contemplating our financial dilemma, I simply stuck my hands into my jean pockets, pulled out the empty pocket liners, and prayed, "Lord, this is what I have to pay Laura's debt—nothing. So, in this moment, I'm giving all of Laura's bills to you. I am giving you the responsibility to provide for her needs."

> God expects us to be responsible stewards of his provisions.

And with that I just quit worrying about the bills. From that moment, in miracle after miracle, every doctor and hospital bill was paid, in full. I never had to worry. God was in charge, and he provided the ways and the means to pay the bills.

Our lack of debt was God's doing. Why did he choose to bless my family this way? One reason is because I released the situation to him. It was his turn, not mine. Besides, trusting God was my only option. I'd no other choice, and the truth is, neither do you.

Let me take this opportunity to grab a tissue and just say, "Thank you, Father."

As president of the ministry Right to the Heart, I plan and present a budget proposal in accordance with our ministry goals to the board every year. It's not uncommon for my proposed budget to be much larger than the previous year's budget.

"Where are the additional funds going to come from?" the board wants to know.

My answer is always the same. "I don't know. All I know is we met every one of our ministry goals last year on a fraction of our approved budget. My proposed budget reflects how much it should cost us to see our new goals come to fruition. However, I propose that we adopt our new goals for the year, but only spend as God provides. If he wants to provide the figure in this budget to help us meet our goals, that's great. But if instead he wants to multiply the little we have to meet our goals, that's great too. I pledge to spend only what we have in our account. Let's vote to accept the budget, only as God provides it. All in favor?"

"Aye!"

It's always unanimous. And no, we never meet our budget goals, though we always pay all our bills and always meet our ministry goals. God multiplies what we do have to accomplish the work he's asked us to complete.

One year I thought we might have an exception to our balanced budget. We were six thousand dollars short of paying our Right to the Heart of Women conference bills because we were inadvertently in conflict with another large women's event. With lower attendance we didn't have enough income to pay our

> God multiplies what we do have to accomplish the work he's asked us to complete.

bills. So, I prayed, "We sought you, Lord, and were absolutely convinced that you wanted us to proceed with our conference in St. Louis. As you know, we're short on our funding. But I'm not going to worry about it. I'm giving you the bills."

But still, things looked grim. In fact, my conference director came to me the evening before our event. "This conference is going to lose a lot of money. Should we just cancel it?"

With confidence, I responded, "No, we're here, we've already spent the money, and we're proceeding ahead. God called us here so he must have a way to provide for our needs. Let's trust him to provide."

We proceeded and had an anointed time with our conferees. A couple of days after the conference, I got a call from one of our speakers who had to bow out of the conference at the last minute because her grandmother was dying. "Linda, thank you for allowing me to hold my grandmother's hand while she slipped into eternity," she said.

"Angela, I knew that's where God wanted you to be, and I'm so glad you were there," I replied.

"Here's the thing," she continued. "My grandmother left me six thousand dollars, and I know she would want me to give it to your ministry."

> One thing we must understand is that God will truly provide all our needs, though he may not provide all our wants.

I was speechless and humbled. Though I hadn't shared our need with Angela, her gift was the exact amount we needed. God provided in such a beautiful and clear way. There was no doubt that he took care of our bills.

Notice one thing about these prayers of relinquishing bills to God. I hadn't taken the ministry credit card and run up large balances in an irresponsible way. I was prayed up. I was absolutely convinced God had called us to St. Louis. And yes, I'd been frugal with the ministry's money.

If you are having financial difficulties because of bad stewardship on your part, read and pray through Karen's story again. Her prayers were answered when she put her budget under God's authority.

But one thing we must understand is that God will truly provide all our needs, though he may not provide all our wants.

However, do we really trust him to provide our needs?

A few years ago I met a remarkable woman named Marva J. Dawn. In her book *Keeping the Sabbath Wholly*, Marva sheds some light on what it truly means to trust God to provide. As she talked about why God commanded us to keep the Sabbath holy, she explained that observing the Sabbath frees us from the need to create our own future. For example, when the Israelites were following Moses through the desert, God told them not to gather manna (bread that fell from heaven) on the Sabbath.

Marva says,

> The point of the whole story is that God will provide for his people; they don't have to struggle to work things out for themselves. Indeed, this is the message throughout the narrative of the Hebrew people—their God will provide for them. . . . He will provide his people with a place to live. He will take them through the Red Sea, across the wilderness, over the Jordan River, and into the Promised Land.[2]

Not only is God our provider, he considers it an insult, a breaking of his commandments, when we don't observe Sabbath and rest in him so that he can provide all our needs.

This means that it's not just us looking for provisions from God; God is looking for opportunities to provide for us without our having to work for it.

When Is Enough Enough?

Greed is one of the biggest problems of this generation. Often, we will ruin our health, our family life, and our marriages just to earn money we don't need to buy things we won't use. Many people live by the creed that "he who dies with the most toys wins." Though perhaps the truth of the matter is he who dies with the most toys is dead and now his toys either belong to others or fill the landfills.

Of course, it's not a sin to be rich, but neither is it a sin to be poor. Proverbs 19:1 says, "Better to be poor and honest than rich and dishonest" (NLT). Proverbs 15:16 adds,

"Better a little with the fear of the LORD than great wealth with turmoil."

If this is true, why is it so hard to be content? Timothy taught a great lesson on this when he said:

> If anyone teaches false doctrines and does not agree to the sound instruction of our Lord Jesus Christ and to godly teaching, he is conceited and understands nothing. He has an unhealthy interest in controversies and quarrels about words that result in envy, strife, malicious talk, evil suspicions and constant friction between men of corrupt mind, who have been robbed of the truth and who think that godliness is a means to financial gain.
>
> But godliness with contentment is great gain. For we brought nothing into the world, and we can take nothing out of it. But if we have food and clothing, we will be content with that. People who want to get rich fall into temptation and a trap and into many foolish and harmful desires that plunge men into ruin and destruction. For the love of money is a root of all kinds of evil. Some people, eager for money, have wandered from the faith and pierced themselves with many griefs.
>
> 1 Timothy 6:3–10

When people who are eager for money try to buy into godliness to build a fatter bank account, their wealth buys them grief.

Personally, I don't want to waste my time earning money to purchase grief. That's a bad deal. Perhaps it's better to learn to be content and forego this kind of senseless quest for wealth.

What about Giving?

This question has become a stumbling stone for many believers for reasons ranging from angry attitudes to small bank accounts. For some, it seems like too big a sacrifice to give 10 percent of everything they own to God.

But for others, the question may be is 10 percent even enough? This amount was set up in the old covenant laws (see Lev. 27:30–33), in the age before grace. For the New Testament says:

> Remember this: Whoever sows sparingly will also reap sparingly, and whoever sows generously will also reap generously. Each man should give what he has decided in his heart to give, not reluctantly or under compulsion, for God loves a cheerful giver. And God is able to make all grace abound to you, so that in all things at all times, having all that you need, you will abound in every good work. As it is written: "He has scattered abroad his gifts to the poor; his righteousness endures forever."
>
> Now he who supplies seed to the sower and bread for food will also supply and increase your store of seed and will enlarge the harvest of your righteousness. You will be made rich in every way so that you can be generous on every occasion, and through us your generosity will result in thanksgiving to God.
>
> 2 Corinthians 9:6–11

Seek God, then cheerfully give as you feel led. However, don't give to get. It's true, there is blessing for those who give, but know that your gift will not necessarily buy you financial gain. Never let an aggressive ministry compel you to give so you can be blessed by God financially. Instead, give because you love God and you feel he's called you to give. If you are even wondering if you are called to give, the answer is yes. But make it a prayer adventure. Seek God and let him show you what to do and who to support. However, don't forget to include your local church. With all this in mind, remember that you can't bribe God, but that you will be blessed when you honor him with your giving.

Let's pray:

Dear Lord,

Thank you for your many provisions. Help me to celebrate a Sabbath day of rest weekly so that you may more fully provide for me.

Please know that all I have is yours. Give me the grace, wisdom, and fortitude needed to be financially obedient, even if it means strict budgeting, tithing, giving in faith, or giving a handout to someone in need. In fact, show me to whom and how much you want me to give and help me to do so with a cheerful heart.

If I have been irresponsible with my finances, show me how to be a better steward of my resources. Bring me to a place of financial solvency and serenity, even if the solution is not a quick fix. All the while, help me to grow up in you.

I bring my current financial crisis before you and ask that you worry about it for me, giving me your wisdom. Show me what to do, one step at a time. I leave this worry and stress at your feet. Give me an obedient heart as I listen for your voice on these matters.

Along with your provision, I pray for contentment with what you have provided. Bring your provisions to my mind, one by one, so that I may thank you more fully for all your blessings and kindnesses to me.

In Jesus' name,
Amen.

Praying Scripture

Dear Lord,

You own the earth and everything and everyone in it. (See Ps. 24:1.)

You meet all of my needs according to the glorious riches in Christ Jesus. (See Phil. 4:19.)

Because time is so short, help me to realize that all I own is not mine to keep. (See 1 Cor. 7:29–31.)

In many cultures I'd be considered rich. Help me not to be arrogant or put my hope in my wealth, but instead, help me to put my hope in you who provides me with everything I need for happiness. (See 1 Tim. 6:17–18.)

Help me to never be so rich that I disown you or so poor that I steal and bring you shame. (See Prov. 30:7–9.)

Your Son taught the disciples not to worry about food or clothes, you who feed the birds and clothe the fields with flowers. If you can do this, I know you can feed and clothe me. For you, heavenly Father, know my needs and take care of them so I can concentrate on living for you. (See Matt. 6:25–33.)

You are my caring shepherd, so I lack for nothing. You give me rest, you restore my soul, and you guide me because you and your name mean love. Because you are with me even in the darkest shadows of life, I will not fear. Your protection is near and you present me with a feast in front of those who wish me evil. You bless me so that my joy overflows. Surely your love and mercy will follow me my entire life and I will one day be with you, forevermore. (See Psalm 23.)

Lord, help me to please you by living my life as a living sacrifice, doing good for others and sharing what I have with those in need. (See Heb. 13:16.)

Helping others is what you've called me to do, for it truly is more blessed to give than to receive. (See Acts 20:35.)

Help me to give to those who ask me for help. (See Matt. 5:42.)

In Jesus' name,
Amen.

9

Praying for Others

If we truly love people, we'll desire for them far more than it is within our power to give them, and this will lead us to prayer: Intercession is a way of loving others.

—Richard J. Foster

One of my favorite church bulletin bloopers reads, "Pray for those who are sick of our church and community." Not only should we pray for these folks, we should pray for whomever God places on our hearts. For prayer is our secret weapon we can use to really do something to help others. The secret is, through prayer, you are tapping into God's great compassion and power on behalf of someone who needs it.

It's clear, God calls us to pray for the sick. James 5:14–15 says, "Is any one of you sick? He should call the elders of the church to pray over him and anoint him with oil in the name of the Lord. And the prayer offered in faith will make the sick person well; the Lord will raise him up. If he has sinned, he will be forgiven."

A couple of years ago I sponsored a small, private retreat for writers in a home in the mountains of Colorado. One of my students was dying of a brain tumor and had arrived ready to learn how to write a book on dying with grace. It was sad. But she was brave and determined good would come from her passing, which her doctors said would occur within the next two years. I helped Beth with her title and outline as we discussed the details of how to best complete and market her book to a publisher.

At the end of the weekend, the students and I gathered in the living room to pray for one another. By this time we all knew each other's secret heartaches, goals, prayer requests, and dreams. When it came time to pray for Beth, I asked her to stand with me in the center of the room while the other women joined us.

Praying in faith means believing God is able.

We all reached out to touch Beth, but I grabbed Beth's arm with both hands. When I closed my eyes to pray, the words I'd planned to say about asking God to give Beth time and grace to finish her project evaporated and were replaced by words that bubbled out of the deep places of my spirit.

I said in a loud voice, "Beth, I'm grabbing you for the kingdom. Maybe I shouldn't pray this prayer, but I can't help it. Beth, I am coming against your brain tumor in the power and authority of Jesus Christ. I say to you, brain tumor, you must leave Beth in the name of Jesus and in the power of his blood and resurrection."

My students, upon hearing these words, got excited. They too prayed against the brain tumor in boldness and power while tears streaked down Beth's cheeks. Several months later, I sent an email to Beth. "How's your book coming along?" I asked.

She wrote back, "Didn't I tell you? After I got home my symptoms started to reverse. When the doctor repeated the tests and the MRI, he discovered the brain tumor was gone. I'm not working on the book on dying, and I couldn't be happier about it."

Wow! Look at what God did. Still, have you ever prayed the prayer of faith for someone who didn't get healed? I have. So, this begs the question, what does praying in faith really mean?

It's simple. As I mentioned earlier, praying in faith means believing God is able.

And what about the promise we read in James that God will raise the sick person up? The original Greek word for raise is *egeirō*. According to *Vine's Expository Dictionary*, *egeirō* has various meanings including being raised up from affliction and the "raising" of the dead. I interpret the latter to also mean rising from death into eternal life. So, the results of a prayer of faith include:

- Being raised from affliction
- Being raised into eternal life or life eternal after death
- Having our sins forgiven

This is all good, but isn't there a way to turn the kind of prayer that brought Beth's healing into a formula that will work for everyone?

Formula? Okay, one of our very first lessons in this book was God does not come with a steering wheel. We can't control him. What we can do is:

- Love him
- Enjoy him
- Fear him

- Walk with him
- Believe him
- Trust him
- Ask of him
- Wait on him

We can do all these things with God, but we cannot *force* him. God once addressed this issue with Moses when he said, "I will have mercy on whom I will have mercy, and I will have compassion on whom I will have compassion" (Exod. 33:19).

Now don't go away thinking you might be the one for whom God has no mercy or compassion. It's a temptation to worry about this, but the very fact that you feel worried indicates that you have a "God connection." The fact that you are interested enough in God to read this book tells me your God-antenna is at least pointed in the right direction. That's a very good sign!

God most often has mercy and compassion on those who draw near to him. The people I worry about have no interest in God, period. Their God antenna is just not operating. If you know someone like this, you can hope God will connect them to his kingdom at some point. In fact, perhaps God himself has called you to be their intercessor.

The people of Israel had a hard time remembering God. In fact, when Moses climbed Mt. Sinai to receive the Ten Commandments from God, the people encamped in the valley below got tired of waiting for his return. They reasoned Moses wasn't coming back and decided to create and worship their own image of God. They fashioned their new god into the shape of a gold calf created from the trinkets given to them by their former captors. Then they began to worship their idol. Can you imagine their audacity? After all they had been through with God, how could they betray him like that?

Especially when you consider God is a jealous God (Exod. 20:4–5). He's not jealous of us, but he's jealous for us to have a committed relationship with him.

We read what happened in Deuteronomy 9 when God told Moses: "I have seen this people, and they are a stiff-necked people indeed! Let me alone, so that I may destroy them and blot out their name from under heaven. And I will make you into a nation stronger and more numerous than they" (v. 13).

Moses could have told God, "You're right. These people don't have a God-antenna like me. I think you should wipe them off the face of the earth; then I'll have you all to myself." Thankfully, Moses didn't respond that way. Instead, through the power of love, he became their intercessor.

Moses fell on the ground and prayed for his people. He later told them,

> Then once again I fell prostrate before the LORD for forty days and forty nights; I ate no bread and drank no water, because of all the sin you had committed, doing what was evil in the LORD's sight and so provoking him to anger. I feared the anger and wrath of the LORD, for he was angry enough with you to destroy you. But again the LORD listened to me.
>
> Deuteronomy 9:18–19

The people didn't deserve it, yet God answered Moses's prayer on their behalf. Why? The Word says, "The prayer of a righteous man is powerful and effective" (James 5:16). Because Moses had a relationship with God, God listened and answered Moses's plea for his people.

Following the Example of Jesus

Now that we're busy making up our prayer list, let's check to see who we've included so far:

1. Our family, church, and community
2. The sick
3. People who need forgiveness

But who else should we add to our list? Perhaps we should see who Jesus prayed for.

All the moms around Jerusalem who were familiar with Jesus' ministry knew he was a great rabbi, perhaps even the long-awaited Messiah. So, they often showed up with their children in tow wherever Jesus preached.

Picture this: with her little one peeking from behind her skirt, a mother tried to steal a moment with Jesus. "Master, could you bless my little Sarah?" Before Jesus could answer, another mom spoke up, "And my sons, Reuben and Josiah?"

With a smile, Jesus gathered these little ones onto his lap and began to pray for them. How sweet. What a moment. The little children looked into the face of Jesus while he looked into the face of his Father.

> According to Jesus we're to pray for the cute, the cuddly, and the horrible.

But the apostles watched and disapproved. They grumbled among themselves, "Who are these women and children to take up the master's precious time? Don't they understand he's on a tight schedule? Who do they think they are?"

One of the disciples crossed his arms and said, "Women, can't you see the master is busy? Now off with you and your little ones."

Jesus paused in his prayer and looked up at his disciples. He said, much to the relief of the shamed mothers, "Let the little children come to me, and do not hinder them, for the kingdom of heaven belongs to such as these" (Matt. 19:14). Jesus smiled down at the children, then closed his eyes and blessed them.

As we discussed earlier, Jesus often prayed for us. But did

he ask us to pray for others? In Luke 6, he gave his great message known as the Beatitudes. He said, "Bless those who curse you, pray for those who mistreat you" (v. 28). If you're like me, praying for kids is much more enjoyable than praying for someone who cursed or hurt me. However, if we follow the example of Jesus, we're to pray for the cute, the cuddly, and the horrible.

So let's add them to our list:

4. Our kids
5. Those who have wronged us

Who Desires Our Prayers?

What if the people on our list don't want our prayers?

They may protest, but deep down I think they are like my friend Cindy. Cindy told me she really doesn't want anything to do with God. Still she says, "If you think about it, would you please, please pray for me?"

I'm guessing you know a few people like Cindy. But even when people say they don't believe in prayer, they are drawn to it in the midst of tragedy. When disasters strike, our airwaves fill with expressions of both faith and prayer. So even though it may be considered politically offensive, public prayer is often cherished in times of trouble as well as times of peace.

A few years ago I was asked to say the lunchtime prayer for a local speakers' group. Though I'm not an ordained minister, I assumed everyone knew I was in ministry. They didn't—as I was about to discover.

I prayed a lovely prayer asking for peace, blessings, and love for everyone in the room. I closed my prayer by saying, "Thank you, Lord, in Jesus' name."

You would have thought a bomb went off. There were angry shouts of "Shalom!"

Didn't that mean peace? Apparently not, as the newly elected president of the organization put his finger in my face and shouted for all to hear: "Get the point?"

I got it all right. There's diversity for everyone—except Christians. At luncheons past, I'd unhappily sat through prayers to Buddha, the Indian spirits, and the universe. But God forbid I pray to Jehovah in the name of Jesus of Nazareth.

A year later, I couldn't believe it when I was asked to pray at the luncheon again until I realized my friend hadn't been at my earlier "prayer bout." So I sweetly smiled and said, "I'd love to."

I prayed the same prayer I'd prayed a year earlier. I prayed for peace, blessings, and love. Then it was time to close the prayer. I paused dramatically, letting the silence hover above the crowd. The people in the room squirmed as they remembered what had happened the year before.

But as I stood quietly before the group, I could feel the presence of the Lord. I knew everyone in the room also sensed his presence and knew to whom I was praying. So I closed my prayer by saying, "Thank you to the Lord who knows who he is."

Laughter and applause erupted. Yes, the Lord knows who he is, and so did my audience who delighted in the fact I'd found a way to acknowledge God despite the oppressive "political correctness" that tried to govern our club.

So let me ask the question again: Who desires our prayers? My audience members did, and so do your friends, neighbors, and family members, whether they realize it or not. So don't be intimidated—add them to your prayer list.

How to Pray

While in New Mexico, I met two sisters who shared how they came to believe in Christ as adults. They had been raised in a large family with ten children. The family believed in God and attended church occasionally, but the children were never taught how they could know God in a personal way through Jesus. In fact, they didn't have a very good opinion of God because their home was riddled with family secrets involving violence and alcoholism.

Their family was in disrepair, filled with pain and hurt. So, when one of their sisters, Victoria, broke with family tradition and got born again, the family took notice. For the most part, however, they were unaffected by the change in Victoria.

Tragically, Victoria developed terminal cancer. It was her dying wish to see her family come to Christ, though she didn't live to see it. After Victoria died, Marie also came to know Jesus as her Savior. Marie began to pray for her parents and all of her brothers and sisters. She prayed for her family as past hurts caused by one or another of her family members came to mind. Each time this happened, Marie asked God to help her forgive that hurt.

Marie said this prayer process took years. Gradually, as she prayed for each family member, she slowly forgave each for the pain of the past. Once she completed this process, she invited her entire family to meet for dinner in a popular restaurant. To her amazement, they all came. After dinner, she invited them to a revival meeting at her church and was surprised when all but one came.

After the preacher presented the gospel of Jesus Christ, he invited audience members who wanted to believe to come forward. Then an amazing thing happened: Marie's family made their way to the front of the church, where they found forgiveness of their sins and a new relationship with God through Christ. Hallelujah!

Marie and her sister say the hound of heaven is now in hot pursuit of the family member who did not attend the revival that night. Marie smiles. "It's just a matter of time. And one day, our entire family will meet on the other side with Jesus and our sister Victoria."

Of course, everyone is individually responsible for how they respond to the gospel, but even so, I'm wondering if our own bitterness could create a roadblock of anger or indifference to those we refuse to forgive? After all, Jesus himself taught us to pray and to say, "And forgive us our sins, just as we have forgiven those who have sinned against us" (Matt. 6:12 TLB).

> We've got to set our hearts right so that others can see the love of Christ.

Therefore, let go of your bitterness and allow God the opportunity to reach his lost sheep through the power of his love and forgiveness in you. We've got to set our hearts right so that others can see the love of Christ.

What are we waiting for? Let's spend some time on our knees. I'll be joining you, praying for all my unsaved loved ones too.

Dear Lord,

By an act of my will, I release _____ from the offense of _____. I give it all to you. I forgive him/her through your power. Please free _____ from any bondage of the enemy so she/he can come to and know you. In addition, Lord, I'm praying for a miracle for _____ with their situation/problem of _____. Please bind the powers of darkness from interfering with this situation, in the mighty name of Jesus. I claim this situation for the kingdom of God.

Lord, I trust you to turn this situation/problem into a miracle.

In Jesus' name,

Amen.

After this prayer, your assignment is to thank God for what he will do and to trust him with the answer, even if it's not the answer you would pick. For we must remember that our ways are not his ways. We can trust that God is working everything out according to his eternal purposes.

> We can trust God to answer our prayers in a way that will do the most eternal good, even when his answers are impossible to understand in the now.

For example, just this weekend I met a mom who lost her two-year-old in a tragic car accident. When she got home from the hospital and walked into his bedroom, she was shocked to see his empty crib. She cried out to the Lord, "Why, Lord, why would you do this to me? Why would you allow my baby to die?"

The Lord gently spoke to her heart, "Even if I told you, you would not be able to understand."

She said this answer to her prayer gave her great comfort in the coming days of grief because, though she might not understand the reason, she could leave it in God's hands. And I think this is a lesson for all of us. God knows the best for us and those we are praying for. For when we allow God to use our tragedies, we will grow in our faith and our dependence on him. We can trust God to answer our prayers in a way that will do the most eternal good, even when his answers are impossible to understand in the now.

When to Pray

We should always be in conversation with God, praying without ceasing. Many people like to have a prayer list, especially if they have a lot of people to pray for. I often use prayer lists, and I think they can be very effective. It's neat to be able to check off each prayer request when it's been answered. Another method I find helpful is if someone asks me to pray, I pray right then and there. After all, why wait? And, I pray each time God brings that person to mind. So, if prayer lists are a good tool for you, please use them. But also try to pray immediately when you are reminded of prayer requests or of someone who might be in need. Sometimes those urgings are most important.

My writing partner for the Potluck Club books, Eva Marie Everson, tells a startling story. It had been a week of late nights, so Eva was not too pleased to wake up at 4:31 in the morning. "Lord, why can't I sleep?" she asked. Immediately the name of a national magazine editor came to mind—Kathleen—someone Eva barely knew. But it seemed God was nudging her to pray for Kathleen.

Pray for focus, the Spirit seemed to direct her heart.

Eva did. The next morning, Eva decided to drop Kathleen a quick email. Kathleen called her right back. She said, "I am almost too astonished to speak!" Kathleen went on to relate that—while Eva was in prayer—she was being stalked on her way to her early morning radio show. She'd dialed 911 into her cell phone but didn't have the courage to press "send." "It was as if the Lord was whispering 'Focus' to me," said Kathleen. And she did focus. She hit send and was rescued as a result.[1]

I love this story. It reminds me that when a person urgently comes to mind, it could be the Father asking us to focus in prayer.

Prayer of Agreement

Sometimes our friends and family may come to us with a difficulty or a prayer request. When that happens, I recommend you immediately stop whatever you're doing and pray. In fact, join them in what I like to call a prayer of agreement. Note, when you include them, you're also including Jesus in your prayer. Matthew 18:19–20 says, "Again, I tell you that if two of you on earth agree about anything you ask for, it will be done for you by my Father in heaven. For where two or three come together in my name, there am I with them." You might also want to jot down this prayer request as a reminder to pray later. Also pray whenever the person or situation comes to mind.

A friend of mine recently fell while he was carrying a large landscaping rock, crushing his arm and severing his tendons. He makes his living working with his hands, so this was a great concern. When I saw him in his cast and bandages, I asked, "Have you ever heard of a prayer of agreement?"

"What's that?"

"That's when you agree with someone, in Jesus' name, for God to answer a prayer request."

"Let's try it," he said.

"What would you like to agree on?"

"Let's agree, in the name of Jesus, that my arm will be totally healed in six weeks. My doctor is saying it will take twelve weeks and that it may never be back to normal."

"I can agree, in Jesus' name, that your arm will be healed in six weeks," I said.

I saw him again five and a half weeks later, this time without his cast or bandages. He said, "I got my cast off yesterday. It's not been quite six weeks, but the doctor says my arm is totally healed. I have no pain, and I'm back at work. My doctor says he's never seen anything like it."

Though my friend has a nasty scar, he says it reminds him that God answered his prayer with a miracle.

Praying Scripture

Dear Lord,

Thank you for my brothers and sisters in you as well as all my loved ones. Father, give them wisdom and revelation so that they may know you better. I pray that the eyes of their hearts may be enlightened so they would know your hope and the riches of your glorious inheritance as well as the incomparably great power you've given to them. (See Eph. 1:15–19.)

Lord, thank you that everything is possible for those who believe. Please help me overcome my unbelief! Thank you that through Jesus I can command the enemy to stop his work among my friends and family members. Help me to be diligent in prayer and fasting to see this work completed by you. (See Mark 9:14–29.)

Lord, I receive your Holy Spirit. I forgive anyone who wronged me so you can forgive me. For Mark 11:25 says, "And when you stand praying, if you hold anything against anyone, forgive him, so that your Father in heaven may forgive you your sins."

In Jesus' name,
Amen.

Now's a great time to start the process of releasing your friends, associates, and family members to God through the power of prayer and forgiveness.

This process may take days, weeks, or even years to complete, but be diligent, especially when you are praying for someone who continues to wound you.

Join me in the next chapter to discuss this question: Can we really trust God with our prayers?

10

Can We Really Trust God with Our Prayers?

If you can't pray a door open, don't pry it open.

—Lyell Rader

How many of us have prayed like this: "Lord, please answer my prayer my way right now." How many times have you prayed, believing God was able, and been unhappy with either his seeming lack of response or an answer you didn't like?

Oh, that we could all pray in faith with the understanding and wisdom that God may be calling us to accept certain situations, both for our good as well as his purposes.

We may not fully know God's purposes because we don't see things from God's point of view. Perhaps, in some cases, it's not our situation that needs to change, it's our perspective.

If we could see a video of our lives from God's perspective, how would we judge the difficulties God has allowed? Yes, God does allow difficulties into our lives. However, it's not necessarily true that he orchestrates them. I say this because some of our difficulties come from the folly of the bad choices or actions of both ourselves and others. Then some of our difficulties come, not from sin or wrong choices, but from the simple fact that again, this is not yet heaven, and sorrow is allowed to roam our land. In fact, sorrow has been known to walk right through our front door. And God allowed it.

> It's no secret to God that you're angry, even if you've hidden your anger from yourself. The good news is God is big enough and loving enough to help you through this emotional pain.

We've touched on God grudges before, but the problem is epidemic. Though a lot of people are angry at God, they often don't like to admit their anger. Dealing with our God grudges is crucial to the health of our faith. If you are starting to feel a bit uncomfortable, don't stop reading. You're about to be set free.

It's no secret to God that you're angry, even if you've hidden your anger from yourself. The good news is God is big enough and loving enough to help you through this emotional pain.

First, if you are angry at God, admit it. You may have trusted God in prayer and feel that he let you down. Then pray this prayer:

Lord,

I admit I have been hurt and angry because you did not seem to answer my prayers. Lord, I lay this hurt and anger at the foot of the cross. I give it up to you. Lord, by an act of my will, I let go of it and ask you to give me the strength to forgive you. I've had a difficult time believing that you love me because of the circumstances you've allowed in my life. Lord, please remove this and every barrier between us so that I can feel your love for me again.

My pain, my anger, my hurt now belong to you. Take the circumstances I've worried about for so long and turn them into good, just as you promised you would. And Lord, when the time is right, show me how you've turned what the enemy meant for evil into a miracle of your love.

In Jesus' name,

Amen.

What a prayer! Take a moment to feel the release in your spirit and to breathe God's love into your soul. For he loves you and he's been waiting for you to let go of these hurts so he can move you forward in his plans and purposes for your life. Take a moment to enjoy this new freedom. Take another moment to thank God in all your circumstances.

This is in accordance with 1 Thessalonians 5:16–18, which says, "Be joyful always; pray continually; give thanks in all circumstances, for this is God's will for you in Christ Jesus." I like the way Eugene Peterson paraphrases this verse in the Message: "Be cheerful no matter what; pray all the time; thank God no matter what happens."

Whoa! Now you may be thinking, *Okay, I can give up my hurt and anger to God, but now you want me to thank him for some of the "junk" I've had to deal with* and *be cheerful about it?*

Yes! Here's the key: no matter what that "junk" is, God has a way to turn it into a blessing. I've mentioned this before, but it's true. Romans 8:28–29 says, "And we know that in all things God works for the good of those who love him, who have been called according to his purpose."

Which things? All things!

My favorite Old Testament story is found in the book of Genesis. I'm going to give you my version of this event, chronicled in Genesis 37, as I envision how it may have happened. This story is about a young boy named Joseph who had a dream—a dream that he would be a great man whose own family would one day respect him and bow before him. His brothers were shepherds, and while they tended sheep, he, their younger brother, got to stay home to study. This was a coveted privilege and opportunity that had been withheld from all but him.

One day, Joseph's father sent him to check on his brothers. They were in a far field watching the flock when they saw Joseph heading their way. He was wearing his coat of many colors, signifying he was their father's favorite. Joseph's brothers burned with envy, for they knew such a coat should have belonged to the oldest of the clan. On many occasions they had reasoned together that the family would be better off without this usurper who not only stole their birthright but their father's affections.

They already had motive to see their brother dead, and now they had opportunity as Joseph walked into their camp. Joseph was met not with friendly handshakes and backslaps but with their fury. Collectively, the brothers seized Joseph with the intent to murder him. They stripped off his coat and shoved and taunted him. As their jeers reached a homicidal pitch, they realized that though they each wanted this brother dead, no one had the guts to bloody their hands. So instead of slitting Joseph's throat, they threw him into a dry well so they could ponder what to do next.

It was a long night for Joseph. As the darkness descended, his whimpers reached his brothers, adding to their worry. What were they going to do? If they gave Joseph his freedom, he would certainly report this incident to their father, and their father would never forgive them. They had to come up with a plan to "dispose" of the boy.

Step back with me for a moment. This was a stunning moment in time—a victory for Joseph, really. If only Joseph could have shared God's perspective, he would have seen this pit was a stepping-stone to destiny.

The next morning, as the sun slid higher into the sky, the sound of a caravan approached. "Help me, please. Someone help me," Joseph called.

And help him these merchants did, gladly paying his brothers a handful of silver, the going rate for a slave. Joseph now had a new destination. The merchants were taking him to the slave auction in Cairo to be sold to the highest bidder. Joseph's hands were bound, and he got a good view of the rear end of a camel as he stumbled across the desert.

> One of the most miraculous things about Joseph's story was his attitude. He stayed cheerful through it all. He worked hard and made the best of every circumstance in which he found himself.

Do you think Joseph praised the Lord through this circumstance? He was probably wondering what he'd done to deserve such terrible betrayal. But if he could have seen his journey from God's perspective, he would have known he was on the road to destiny.

Once in Egypt, Joseph was purchased by a wealthy family. However, when he refused to bed his mistress, in a revengeful rage she accused him of attempted rape. Joseph was thrown into prison without mercy, parole, or even the hope of freedom. Once again, Joseph probably did not recognize that God was at work, preparing him to be in a position of power.

Still, one of the most miraculous things about Joseph's story was his attitude. He stayed cheerful through it all. He worked hard and made the best of every circumstance in which he found himself.

And Joseph's dreams were about to come true. God was about to use Joseph's hopeless circumstance to give hope to the nations. Joseph was about to have two new visitors who would change his life. These visitors were from the royal court of Pharaoh himself. No one is sure what happened in Pharaoh's court that day, except that the royal wine taster and the royal baker must have made a royal mistake because they were both tossed into prison. It's no wonder these two had bad dreams that night. And it's no surprise that a godly man like Joseph divinely interpreted their dreams. To the wine taster, Joseph explained, "About your dream, don't worry. In three days you'll be back serving the king." But to the baker, Joseph said, "Sorry, your news is bad. The pharaoh will soon see you dead. You will be hung by the neck, a feast for the birds."

Just as Joseph predicted, the pharaoh sprung the butler but strung up the cook. Two years later, the pharaoh himself began to experience disturbing nightmares that no one in his court could interpret.

That's when his wine taster said, "Sire, back in prison I met a guy who could interpret my dreams. If this man could explain my dream, could it be that he could explain yours?"

So when Pharaoh called Joseph to his court, he told Joseph his dreams about skinny cows eating fat cows and skinny stalks of corn eating fat stalks. But it was God who gave Joseph the dream's meaning. Joseph explained, "In seven years there will be a great famine that will sweep the land. You'll need to find a wise man who can oversee the storage of grain so that your people will have food when the land is parched and barren."

The pharaoh replied, "I think I see that wise man standing before me now. It's you, Joseph. You will make the necessary preparations for the famine. Here's my ring to wear. You will be in charge, answering only to me."

What a sweet conclusion to a journey that had been created out of evil, envy, attempted murder, betrayal, lies, and false imprisonment. Who would have thought this journey of Joseph's, so obviously inspired by the evil one himself, would usher this young man to the throne room of Egypt to become second in command to the pharaoh himself? Only God.

When the famine struck, Joseph's starving brothers came to Egypt to buy grain. These brothers didn't recognize their brother when they bowed at his feet because he looked so different. He now had a few years behind him, possibly a shaven head, and perhaps a bit of blue eye makeup. He was also called by a different name—"Sire."

> "Don't be afraid. Am I in the place of God? You intended to harm me, but God intended it for good to accomplish what is now being done, the saving of many lives."

How could the brothers have known they were bowing before Joseph?

Just imagine, Joseph could have given the command to the royal guard, "Off with the heads of these evil men! They betrayed me and now they must pay."

When he revealed his identity to his brothers, they must have thought, "We're dead!" But to their relief, Joseph spoke these remarkable words found in Genesis 50:19–20: "Don't be afraid. Am I in the place of God? You intended to harm me, but God intended it for good to accomplish what is now being done, the saving of many lives."

Joseph's story is an example of why we can be thankful while trusting God through difficulties. God intends to use our difficulties for good. Still, does this concept of thanking God for all circumstances apply to you? Absolutely. Try it. Thank God for your circumstances, then step out of the way and watch God move despite and through your circumstances.

There's no need to despair. God has a plan for your life, a plan that the enemy cannot destroy. Whatever foul ball the enemy pitches your way, God will turn into a home run for the kingdom and for you.

Just as Satan thought he'd defeated Christ on the cross, God used the cross to defeat Satan's power of sin and death. Satan can't win! Our circumstances, even when created by the evil one, will only serve to defeat him. They will only serve to make us victorious.

The apostle Paul said in Philippians 4:11–13, "I have learned to be content whatever the circumstances. I know what it is to be in need, and I know what it is to have plenty. I have learned the secret of being content in any and every situation, whether well fed or hungry, whether living in plenty or in want. I can do everything through him who gives me strength."

Bottom line: it's all about trusting God.

Several years ago, my husband flew my son and me in a Cessna 210 (that's a small plane) to Texas to spend Thanksgiving with our families. Sadly, we always have to leave our precious Laura behind with trusted caregivers as Laura cannot travel great distances because of her care needs.

However, after a wonderful reunion with our loved ones and eating our fill of pie and turkey, we hopped back into the plane to return to our home in Colorado.

It was a lovely morning. The rains from the day before had left the air sweet and clear. Soon we reached ten thousand feet, eye level with an occasional fluffy cloud. The hum of the plane's engine droned on as I studied the tiny farmhouses and irrigated circles of crops so far below us.

Suddenly the droning stopped, and we glided in silence. I turned to Paul, my hubby-pilot. "Is this bad?" I asked.

Beads of sweat popped on his brow. "Yes. I've got to find a place for an emergency landing."

Suddenly the engine sputtered back to life, but before I could breathe a sigh of relief, it died again. I felt my blood drain from my face. I turned to the back seat, where our ten-year-old son sat totally undisturbed and reading a book. "Pray, Jimmy. Pray!" I said.

He looked up briefly. "Okay," he said nonchalantly.

The plane continued to sputter. "Where are you going to land?" I asked Paul.

"We're only fifty miles out of Waco, and they have a great repair shop there. I'm going to try to make it in," he replied. "Cessnas can glide for miles."

I thought I might pass out. Paul expected us to glide with no engine power for fifty miles? I closed my eyes to beseech heaven for help.

As soon as my eyes shut, I saw a vision of Jesus. He was like a tower. His feet were on the earth and his face was in the clouds. His hand was cupped around our little plane floating through the air.

"You are in the palm of my hand," he whispered to my spirit. "You couldn't be safer."

You'd think that this unexpected vision of Jesus during this emergency situation would have given me peace. But the fear I felt was overwhelming. "It would really help me trust you, Lord, if the engine would stay on," I told him.

But it continued to sputter, pause, and glide for mile upon mile. The next thing I knew, we were coming into the Waco airport. Just as our wheels touched down, the engine froze once again. We rolled to a stop in the middle of the runway.

The tower called on the radio: "Cessna, you are in harm's way. Please exit the runway now."

"I'd like to, but our engine has died. We'll need a tow," Paul replied to the tower operator.

They had to close the runway while they hooked our plane to a motorized cart and tugged us to safety. Suddenly, as we were being towed, one of our wheels popped off the plane and the metal wheelbase dug into the pavement. *Lord*, I prayed, *what if that had happened when we were landing? We would have flipped end over end.* Despite my pounding heart, I felt the Lord's smile. "I was with you. You have never been safer."

In the days and years since that moment, I have often thought of the words I heard during our crisis. Those words are still true. When God is with us, we couldn't be safer.

When Noah and his family were in a great flood that wiped out the unbelieving people of their land, they were safe (see Genesis 6–9). When Daniel was tossed in the lions' den for an entire night, he was safe (see Daniel 6). When Shadrach, Meshach, and Abednego were thrown into the fiery furnace because they would not bow down and pray to King Nebuchadnezzar, they were safe (see Daniel 3). And, despite the fact that even the guards who threw them into the fire died from the heat, the king saw there was a fourth man with them. And who do you suppose that man was? It was the Lord himself.

When you trust God and live your life for him, he will be with you in trouble. Let's take a look at what Shadrach, Meshach, and Abednego said to King Nebuchadnezzar just before they got "fired" in the kiln.

Furious with rage, Nebuchadnezzar summoned Shadrach, Meshach, and Abednego and said to them, "Is it true that you do not serve my gods or worship the image of gold I have set up? Now when you hear my theme music, you should fall down and worship the image I made. But if you do not, you will be thrown immediately into a blazing furnace. Then what god will be able to rescue you from my hand?" (Dan. 3:13–15, paraphrased).

Shadrach, Meshach, and Abednego replied to the king, "O Nebuchadnezzar, we do not need to defend ourselves before you in this matter. If we are thrown into the blazing furnace, the God we serve is able to save us from it, and he will rescue us from your hand, O king. But even if he does not, we want you to know, O king, that we will not serve your gods or worship the image of gold you have set up" (Dan. 3:16–18).

This is a striking, faith-filled response. These three Hebrews were saying in effect, "We love God so much we'll lay down our lives for him. We believe he is able to spare us, but even if he doesn't, we'll not dishonor him."

> If only we could view our troubles from this perspective. If only we could say, "Lord, I will not dishonor you. And if you want me to go into the furnace, I will go. I know you are capable of saving me, but to honor you I will face and even embrace the circumstance you've allowed in my life."

If only we could view our troubles from this perspective. If only we could say, "Lord, I will not dishonor you. And if you want me to go into the furnace, I will go. I know you are capable of saving me, but to honor you I will face and even embrace the circumstance you've allowed in my life."

If you can pray this, when others peer into the fire they will see that you are not consumed. They will see Jesus standing in the circumstance with you. If you love and trust God that much, I challenge you to pray so. Remember that trusting God is a journey. All you have to do is to take it one step, one day, at a time.

One summer day, long before we had children, Paul and I and a group of friends hiked into a hidden valley in the Sangre De Cristo mountain range in southern Colorado.

This beautiful valley contained a glassy lake surrounded by rugged fourteen-thousand-foot mountain peaks. We pitched our tents in a wildflower-filled meadow near the edge of a pine forest, planning the next day's climbing adventures.

Paul was set to climb the magnificent but deadly Crestone Needle with several experienced mountaineers. The Needle, a 14,197-foot vertical piece of jagged rock jutting from the earth, could only be conquered with climbing ropes and crampons. My friend Linda and I decided to go for the more demure 14,064-foot Humbolt Peak, which had a clearly marked hiking trail. "Perfect," I decided. "No hanging on ropes for me!"

But as Linda and I began to trudge up Humbolt's steep path, I could see the mountain was more challenging than I'd realized. The wind was blowing a cold chill through my body, and the trail was steeper than I imagined. I decided it wasn't truly a trail at all but an alpine slide. If a pebble rolled beneath my foot and I slipped, there was nothing to stop my fall. Fear began to conquer me, and as we neared the boulder field ahead, I froze in my tracks. "I can't go on, Linda," I admitted. "I feel I'm going to fall."

"Can you walk back down?" Linda asked. I swallowed a lump in my throat. "No, I'm stuck," I said.

"Linda, I have good news for you. All you have to do is take the next step. Can you do that?"

"Yes," I said hesitantly, and I did. "Now what?"

"Now, all you have to do," Linda told me, "is to take the next step."

The next thing I knew, one step at a time, I found the top of the mountain peak.

I discovered the breathtaking view was worth all my effort. An ocean of fourteen-thousand-foot peaks nestled in billows of fluffy clouds lay before me. But best of all, I'd

> If you want a mountaintop experience, if you want to rise above your life's circumstances, God is probably not going to send you an elevator. He will simply walk with you, guiding you one step at a time.

overcome my fear! Linda and I'd made it to the top, just by taking one step after the other.

The same is true with your circumstances. You don't have to analyze the entire journey ahead. All you have to do is concentrate on the next step, then the next, and then the next. If you want a mountaintop experience, if you want to rise above your life's circumstances, God is probably not going to send you an elevator. He will simply walk with you, guiding you one step at a time.

You may find pitfalls, difficult hand-over-hand climbs, cliff-hangers, and even bolts of lightning along the way, but all you have to do is stay connected to God. Then, with and through him, take the next step, rejoicing that your journey has a purpose and that you're not alone. The Lord of the universe is with you, in the pits, in the fire, and on the mountaintops.

Are you ready to pray? Before you respond, answer this: do you trust what you can do with your life more than what God can do? I'll tell you one thing, I'd much rather trust in God than in myself. Take the next step with God with this prayer:

Lord,

I will not dishonor you. And if you want me to go into the furnace, I will go. I know you are capable of saving me, but to honor you I will face and even embrace the circumstances you've allowed in my life.

Lord, help me in this situation. I know you have the power to change the circumstances, and I'm asking that you do so. However, I submit to your will, your ways, and your purposes.

In Jesus' name,

Amen.

Praying Scripture

Dear Lord,

You say that if I ask, it will be given to me; if I seek, I will find; if I knock, the doors will be opened to me. Even my own father would not give me a rock if I asked him for bread nor would he give me a snake if I asked him for fish. And you, Father, are more loving and holy than my earthly father. You know how to give me good gifts when I ask you. (See Matt. 7:7–12.)

Lord, you reign forever, you judge in righteousness and with justice. You are a refuge for the oppressed, a stronghold in times of trouble. Because I know your name, I will trust in you, for you, Lord, have never forsaken me when I've sought you. (See Ps. 9:7–10.)

I will trust in your unfailing love, and my heart rejoices in your salvation. I will sing to you, for you have been good to me. (See Ps. 13:5–6.)

I know you have anointed me and you will save me. You answer me from your holy heaven with the saving power of your right hand. Though some will trust in their bank account and possessions, I will trust in your name, Lord. (See Ps. 20:6–7.)

In Jesus' name,

Amen.

11

Why God Answers

All who call on God in true faith, earnestly from the heart, will certainly be heard, and will receive what they have asked and desired, although not in the hour or in the measure, or the very thing which they ask. Yet they will obtain something greater and more glorious than they had dared to ask.

—Martin Luther

Yes, it's true God answers prayer. But have you ever wondered why? The best answers may be what I call the top ten reasons God answers our prayers:

1. Because he hears us
2. To let us know he is God
3. Because he loves us
4. Because he knows our names
5. To let others know we belong to him
6. Because he is gracious and merciful
7. To turn hearts to him
8. To turn people from false gods

9. To turn us from sin
10. For his glory

Most of these reasons are demonstrated in the story of Elijah. The year was 922 BC, and Elijah was God's prophet. When Ahab became the king of Israel, he took the royal princess Jezebel from the neighboring kingdom of Zidonia to be his bride. As a wedding present, Ahab built Jezebel an altar and temple to her god, Baal. This was a horrific thing in the eyes of God. Not only did Ahab present a false god to the people of Israel but the very acts of Baal worship were abominable.

For example, the people—men, women, and probably older children—engaged in a sexual orgy as an act of worship. This often resulted in unwanted pregnancies, which fueled the practice of baby sacrifices, a sacred fertility ritual. In this ghastly act of Baal worship, the priests would heat the metal idol of Baal with a blazing fire built into its belly. Then they would place the sacrificial baby into the belly or into the idol's arms to be burned alive as the mother as well as the people looked on. Reportedly the people sang loud worship songs in an effort to drown out the screams of the dying child.

> Our God does not require us to sacrifice our children to him; instead, he sacrificed his son for us.

Unbelievably wicked. Aren't you glad we don't serve a God like that? Our God does not require us to sacrifice our children to him; instead, he sacrificed his Son for us.

Consider this: could it be that our God is a jealous God because he loves us and wants to protect us from this kind of demonic misery and heartache?

What suffering the people, especially the women and their daughters, must have endured. I can hardly imagine being handed off by my father or husband to other men, then having my resulting child ripped from my arms to die such a gruesome death while I looked on.

It's unthinkably tragic.

It was no big surprise that God was not pleased. He sent his prophet Elijah to give King Ahab a wake-up call. God's prophet told the king there would be no dew or rain until he, Elijah, said so. With that said, Elijah disappeared into the wilderness. Three years later, after terrible drought and famine, God called Elijah back to the court of Ahab. As Elijah stood before the king, Ahab asked, "Aren't you the man who troubles Israel?"

Elijah answered, "It's not me. It's you for forsaking God's law and following Baal." Then Elijah said, "I challenge you to a contest, Ahab. My God against yours."

Ahab agreed because with his 450 prophets of Baal against the Lord God, Jehovah, and his lone prophet Elijah, the odds seemed to be in his favor. The terms of the contest? The winning and true god would cause fire to fall to burn the sacrifice laid upon his altar. Winner take all.

On the chosen day, Elijah pointed a bony finger at the gathered crowd as his voice thundered, "How long will you waver between two beliefs? If the Lord is God, follow him; if Baal, follow him."

As the people watched in silence, the prophets of Baal began their ceremony. They placed the body of a bull on their altar, and then from morning till the time for evening sacrifice, they called to Baal to consume their offering with fire. Despite their desperate attempts of pleading, dancing, and cutting themselves till their clothes were red with their own blood, their god did not respond.

Elijah mocked them. "Shout louder. Maybe Baal is sleeping or maybe he went to relieve himself." Finally around sunset,

Elijah called to the people to gather around him. He built an altar and dug a trench around it. Next, he had four barrels of water dumped over the sacrificial bull, altar, and trenches. Once this was done, he called for the barrels to be refilled and emptied a second and third time.

When the altar, wood, and the sacrifice were soaked with water, Elijah called out to God: "O LORD, God of Abraham, Isaac and Israel, let it be known today that you are God in Israel and that I am your servant and have done all these things at your command. Answer me, O LORD, answer me, so these people will know that you, O LORD, are God, and that you are turning their hearts back again" (1 Kings 18:36–37).

While his words still echoed in the ears of the people, a deafening roar rocked the altar as Elijah's sacrifice erupted into flames, even licking the water from the trenches. At first, the people stood motionless, feeling the heat of the blaze flicker upon their faces. Then as one they fell on their faces and cried, "The Lord he is God! The Lord he is God!"

The Israelite men turned into an army. At Elijah's command, the 450 prophets of the false god Baal suddenly became extinct within the land. At last, the wives, daughters, and children of the Israelite men were safe and in the protection of Jehovah, the one true God; the God who had saved them from worshiping a lie.

This story demonstrates the top ten reasons I believe God answers our prayers. How? It shows God answered Elijah's prayer, not only because he knew Elijah by name but to demonstrate his glory and power. God's response helped his people recognize him and turn from their sins, turn from worshipping a false god, and turn their hearts back to God. God answered Elijah's prayers and will answer our prayers as well, even though we don't deserve it. We're sinners, after all. Yet, God hears even our groanings as prayers. We read in Acts

7:33–34: "Then the Lord said to him, 'Take off your sandals; the place where you are standing is holy ground. I have indeed seen the oppression of my people in Egypt. I have heard their groaning and have come down to set them free.'"

While speaking at a conference one weekend in Texas, a woman pulled me aside to tell me her story. It seems she'd been in a jewelry store when masked gunmen entered the building. Terri knew from reading the papers that these thugs left no survivors. After scooping the diamonds and jewelry into their knapsacks, one of the robbers held a gun to Terri's head and said, "Are you ready to meet the Lord?"

Terri groaned and nodded. Though her voice trembled, she answered, "I am."

The gunman said, "I know you are. You made the same groaning sound that all the Christians have made, right before I've shot them in the head."

But before the robber could pull the trigger, the S.W.A.T. team dropped from the ceiling and Terri and the other hostages were saved.

Terri asked me, "Do you think the groan I made was a prayer?"

Absolutely. Romans 8:26–27 says, "In the same way, the Spirit helps us in our weakness. We do not know what we ought to pray for, but the Spirit himself intercedes for us with groans that words cannot express. And he who searches our hearts knows the mind of the Spirit, because the Spirit intercedes for the saints in accordance with God's will."

These verses remind me of the wise words of my friend's eight-year-old granddaughter. The family was facing a crisis, and that night at bedtime prayers, my friend said, "Sweetheart, I can't even find the words to pray over our troubles."

Her granddaughter replied, "That's okay, God can read our hearts."

There is an old joke about the dad who passed his daughter's bedroom one night as she recited the alphabet in an oddly reverent way.

"What are you doing?" the dad asked.

"Praying," the daughter answered. "But I can't think of the right words, so I'm just saying all the letters so God will put them together for me."

John Bunyan once said, "In prayer it is better to have a heart without words than words without heart."[1] Even when your words are spent, God's Holy Spirit prays for you.

Hearing God's Voice

You'd think after God's fire had consumed his offering and after the prophets of Baal no longer practiced their evil upon the people, Elijah would rise victorious, the man of the hour who had a direct hotline to God himself.

Instead, when he heard Queen Jezebel wanted him dead, he ran back into the wilderness alone. Eventually he made his way to Mount Horeb and hid in a cave. The word of the Lord came to him: "What are you doing here, Elijah?"

Elijah practically blubbered, "After all I've done for you and the people, they want me dead."

God answered, "Come and stand on the mountain."

Elijah did and braced himself against a violent wind that sent boulders crashing down the mountainside. But God was not in the wind.

Then came a jolting earthquake. But God was not in the earthquake.

Then came a consuming fire. But God was not in the fire.

After the fire, there was a gentle voice. "What are you doing here, Elijah?"

God was in the voice. In that quiet moment, God gave Elijah brand-new marching orders, which included the orders to anoint a new king. God still had a purpose for Elijah, and because Elijah had been faithful to rid the land of the false god, a new day had dawned for God's people.

I love this story, and I love the fact that God answered Elijah, not in the wind, the earthquake, or the fire, but in his still, small voice.

If you are a believer, if the spirit of God indwells your soul, then you've heard that voice. Maybe you didn't understand to whom it belonged. Perhaps it came as a little thought that seemed to bubble from your heart. Then again, maybe you've felt it as a gentle smile of love. Perhaps you heeded it, or maybe you pushed it aside.

The key is learning to recognize his voice. Recognizing his voice is something I strive daily to do. And as you learn to listen for God's voice, it will become more familiar and easier to recognize. Listening for God's voice was the one thing God himself called Elijah to do. And yes, God's sweet, still voice still whispers to us, his people. It comes in quiet urgings, thoughts, and moments of prayer. It comes as we spend time reading his Word.

Unfortunately, the voice of God has some competition, which can make it hard to hear and harder to recognize. God's voice competes against the voices of entertainments, the media, busyness, the temptations and whispers of the evil one, and our very own selfish thoughts and desires. So how can we know when and if we've really heard from God?

How God Speaks to Us

There are several ways God speaks to us today, including his Word, his still, small voice, opportunities, burdens, others, divine intervention, and his creation. Let's look at these one by one.

The Word

Reading the Bible daily gives God the opportunity to speak directly into your life. You'll discover the Scripture you need for an important decision or the answer to a question is readily available when you open the Word. Why does this happen? Because the Word is living and sharper than a two-edged sword (see Heb. 4:12).

Pray this each time you open your Bible: "Dear Lord, please speak to me through your Word. Open the eyes of my understanding."

Then, eagerly contemplate the words before you. You'll meet him as you spend time abiding in his Word. Give God this opportunity to speak to you through his Word daily. If you are new to the practice of daily Bible reading, start with the book of John, then move on to other New Testament books before digging into the Old Testament. I enjoy listening to the Bible on tape and CD on my car stereo while I'm running my errands. If you can't afford your own set, your local library should be able to lend one to you.

His Still, Small Voice

Practice a daily time of waiting on the Lord. My favorite time to do this is when I'm just waking up. My own thoughts are not yet crowding my mind, so his voice is easier to hear. I quietly pray as I awaken, "Lord, I love you. Do you have anything to say to me today?"

Then I wait. Sometimes, I drift back into sleep only to be awakened by the buzz of my alarm clock, while other times

I feel his sweet presence as his gentle voice says, "I love you, my daughter."

As I listen, God might whisper to my heart something he wants me to do or some lesson he wants me to learn. My biggest struggle is not to interrupt him, peppering him with comments and questions, but to keep listening. For it's in my quiet waiting that he speaks.

I know I've heard from God when I feel his loving presence and when the words I hear do not conflict with the teachings of the Bible or instruct me to break one of God's Ten Commandments (see Exod. 20:1–17).

I test the spirit by asking, "Lord, is that really you?" I wait for his answer, and then ask, "Are you the Lord who sent his Son to die on the cross and to rise from the dead as a payment for my sin?" Then again, I wait for his answer, which often feels like a warm smile in my soul.

Why do I ask such questions? Because if the enemy is trying to speak to me in a counterfeit voice, he will flee before he acknowledges Jesus. First John 4:1–3 says,

> Dear friends, do not believe every spirit, but test the spirits to see whether they are from God, because many false prophets have gone out into the world. This is how you can recognize the Spirit of God: Every spirit that acknowledges that Jesus Christ has come in the flesh is from God, but every spirit that does not acknowledge Jesus is not from God. This is the spirit of the antichrist, which you have heard is coming and even now is already in the world.

Don't fret if God does not speak to you in this way. There's no shame in it at all. He doesn't speak to everyone the same way. However, give him the opportunity by practicing his presence, listening, and waiting quietly on him.

Opportunities

As believers we often refer to opportunities as open doors or windows. However, be careful not to confuse every open door with God's leading, for the gate to hell is wide open too. Practice discernment. Dictionary.com defines discernment as "the act or process of exhibiting keen insight and good judgment." And pray! Ask God, "Are you leading me in this direction? Please make it clear."

For example, what if you had the opportunity to have an extramarital affair at work? Does this opportunity mean this is an open door you should take? Of course not! The Word says, "You shall not commit adultery" (Exod. 20:14). The temptation you are facing is not God calling you to sin. God will never, never call you to go against any of his commandments. Ever.

But let's say your pastor calls and asks you to teach in the three-year-old Sunday school class. This may be an opportunity set up for you by the Lord, or then again maybe not. This is where prayer and discernment come in. Did you ask God to give you an opportunity to serve at church? Do you have the availability? Do you love teaching children about God? If one or more of the answers to these questions is yes, then this opportunity may indeed be from the Lord.

But again, pray and utilize discernment.

Burdens

God may burden you with the vision of a need in order to awaken you to take more responsibility in his kingdom. And if you're not clear what I mean, let me ask you a question. Have you noticed a hole at your church or in your community that you wish the pastor or someone would fill? Here's the question you must pray through—is God giving you the burden because he's calling you to pray, calling you into service, or both? You can find out. Pray and ask him to show you.

Others

Pay close attention to the recommendations of others.

During a panel at our Right to the Heart of Women Conference, one of the attendees asked, "I'm doing God's work at church, but my husband wants me to spend more time with him and the family. How can I get him off my back so I can do what I'm called to do?"

The panel answered much to the surprise of the conferee, "We're not telling you not to minister at church, but God is calling you to minister to your husband and your children first."

In other words, God was using the words of her husband (and the panel) to let her know she needed to take care of her responsibilities at home. However, let me give you a word of caution. Please use your discernment. Take note if you receive counsel that gives you a check in your spirit. Don't get me wrong, I'm not saying you should toss out the advice just because you don't care for it. But a true check in your spirit indicates a warning that this counsel is not of God.

For example, when I was seventeen, a young man called me out of the blue and said, "God told me to get married, so I decided to call and ask you to be my wife."

With those words I received a big check in my spirit, so I answered, "Well, I'm sorry. God hasn't told me to marry you, and unless he does, I'll have to say thank you, but no."

What if I had assumed his "God told me" statement was really of God? I could have entered into a disaster of heart and soul. Several years later I did indeed marry the man God called me to marry, and there was no check in my spirit. We *both* knew it was right. That meant there were two witnesses to the truth.

There is great wisdom in that. Seek out more witnesses to corroborate the advice or recommendations you've received, especially if you're in doubt (see 2 Cor. 13:1). Ask God to send someone to help you verify or disqualify the recommendation. Also, search the Word to see if Scripture contradicts the counsel you receive.

Beware of any advice you receive that goes against God's Word. That's a sure sign this advice is off base. Never follow such recommendations.

One last thing, be careful not to rely on others more than you rely on God. That's co-dependence, and you need to be careful not to fall into that trap. God is your number one support! His greatest desire is to see you make the right choices for a successful life!

Divine Intervention

God is God, and he knows how to get our attention. Remember the story of the Texas gang members who demanded I prove there was a God? Well, as it turns out, I didn't have to prove anything. God swirled the wind and flashed the lightning himself.

Though you are powerless to make God perform a miracle, you can completely give the situation to him in prayer: "Lord, this is your problem. Now it's your turn." You can thank him for his provision in advance: "Lord, thank you for providing for all my needs and taking care of this problem."

Then wait on God. David understood the principle of waiting. He wrote laments like the one found in Psalm 27:7–14.

> Hear my voice when I call, O LORD;
>> be merciful to me and answer me.
> My heart says of you, "Seek his face!"
>> Your face, LORD, I will seek.
> Do not hide your face from me,
>> do not turn your servant away in anger;
>> you have been my helper.
> Do not reject me or forsake me,
>> O God my Savior.
> Though my father and mother forsake me,
>> the LORD will receive me.
> Teach me your way, O LORD;
>> lead me in a straight path
>> because of my oppressors.
> Do not turn me over to the desire of my foes,
>> for false witnesses rise up against me,
>> breathing out violence.
>
> I am still confident of this:
>> I will see the goodness of the LORD
>> in the land of the living.
> Wait for the LORD;
>> be strong and take heart
>> and wait for the LORD.

His Creation

In the story of Elijah, God was not in the wind, the earthquake, or the fire. God is not his creation. He holds it together—he is before all things, and in him all things hold together (see Col. 1:17).

God is not the actual rainbow, the wind, or the mountain view; instead, he's the Creator of it all. We are not God or his creation the universe, but we can enjoy his handiwork. And while we enjoy the beauty of his immense creation, we may feel his sweet presence.

However, in no way should enjoying God's creation substitute for basking in the sweet fellowship of his people at your local church. Keep your balance and keep the faith.

The Counterfeit Voice

We do have an enemy, and he speaks. How will you recognize his voice? He's the author of lies and he uses his voice to whisper messages of fear, doubt, discouragement, hurt, and panic. Common phrases most often whispered into our minds by the enemy include:

- Who do you think you are?
- You're stupid.
- You can't do that.
- No one cares. (In fact, no one's even going to come to your funeral!)
- You're not making a difference.
- You should give up.
- You're going to lose your [job, marriage, kids, etc.].
- Your circumstances are impossible. God can't be in them, use them, or change them.

I'm sure you're familiar with this voice. Here's what to do when you hear it: tell that old liar to "be quiet, in the name of Jesus." I heard the enemy whisper audibly to me in the middle of the night when my son was a baby. It was about 11:00 p.m. and I'd been up with Jim. I climbed into bed and stared at the ceiling for a few minutes. In the stillness, a voice suddenly whispered aloud, "Who do you think you are?"

I knew this voice was not from my loving heavenly Father, and I said into the darkness: "I am a daughter of the king, and I rebuke you in the name of Jesus." As soon as I said these words, the voice hissed back what sounded like cursing in a language I couldn't understand.

The next morning, my friend Marcia stopped by and told me, "I had the strangest experience last night."

"I did too. What happened to you?"

"I was asleep when a voice whispered into one of my ears, 'Who do you think you are?' I told it to leave in Jesus' name," she said.

"What time was that?" I asked.

"About 11:00 p.m.," she said.

"Well, your little friend came over to my house and said the same thing to me."

So the enemy can speak and you can recognize him by what he has to say. If you should hear him, don't be afraid; just use the power of the name of Jesus to tell him to leave you alone.

Praying Scripture

Dear Lord,

You promise if I hear your words and put them into practice, I am like a wise man who built his house on the rock. The rains and floods cannot destroy it. But if I ignore your words, I am like a foolish man who built his house on the sands. When the rains and flood came, his house was swept away. Help me, Father, to build my house on you. (See Matt. 7:24–27.)

It's those who don't just hear your commands, Lord, but obey them who are considered righteous. (See Rom. 2:13–14.)

Help me not only to listen to your Word but to do it. Otherwise I'm like a man who looks into a mirror and then forgets what he looks like. Help me instead be like the man who looks into your Word and law and obeys it. For obeying your Word is where I will find true freedom and blessings. (See James 1:22–25.)

Help my heart to fear and respect you, O Lord, so I will keep your commands and all may go well with my children and my household. (See Deut. 5:28–29.)

In Jesus' name,
Amen.

12

Our Response

Everyone has heard about your obedience, so I am full of joy over you; but I want you to be wise about what is good, and innocent about what is evil.

—Romans 16:19

What would happen if you got your marching orders from God but refused them? What a terrible thought. When you've heard from God, prayed it through, and know your marching orders don't conflict with Scripture, yet you refuse to do his bidding, what happens then? At the very least you'll quench God from speaking into your life.

If you get a check in your spirit about a TV show you are watching, a DVD you want to rent, something you start to put in your shopping cart, or that high-fat food item you are ordering at the fast food restaurant, you'd better pay attention. Stop and pray, then move the way you think God is leading you. Otherwise, you'll grieve the voice of the Holy Spirit when he tries to speak to you. If you fail to listen, his voice will grow faint or even silent.

I believe we are moving into a time when we need to hear his voice more than ever. Turning a deaf ear to him could prove disastrous for you and your family. Deuteronomy 5:32–33 says, "So be careful to do what the LORD your God has commanded you; do not turn aside to the right or to the left. Walk in all the way that the LORD your God has commanded you, so that you may live and prosper and prolong your days in the land that you will possess."

We know we're supposed to obey the Ten Commandments and follow God's Word. But what do you do when the Lord tells you to do something specific but you're afraid to do it?

A few months after our frightening landing in the small plane in Waco, Texas, I determined I would never be a passenger in a small plane again. Until the Lord woke me from a deep sleep and whispered to my spirit, "Get back into the plane with Paul."

"Lord, is that you?"

The presence of his loving spirit was my confirmation as he whispered, "When you are in the palm of my hand, you couldn't be safer." The Lord had indeed spoken to me. I sat up in bed. *Why would the Lord give me such a terrifying task?* I wondered. Despite our previous safe landing, I still felt shaken. This was something I had to think about, pray about, and ponder as I waited for the next family plane trip.

After much wrestling in my spirit, I finally decided that if God told me to get in the plane, I'd be safer there than anywhere else. The clincher for me was an experience I'd had a couple of years earlier. As I was driving to a speaking engagement in the Colorado town where I live, I looked up to see a small plane heading for the same spot on the road where I happened to be driving. The pilot was coming in for an emergency landing and couldn't see me. There was no way to drive to safety, and I thought, *How will they ever explain to my mom I was killed in a small plane crash while driving my car?*

However, at the last second, the pilot of the small plane did see the power line he was also about to hit and was able to pull out of his descent and circle around the roadway. By the time he did crash land, I was a mile down the road. Thankfully, no one was hurt, including me.

Fully understanding that I could die in a small plane crash anywhere, I decided if I were to die, I'd rather die while being obedient.

> If you want God to move on your behalf, you must choose to follow his lead, or the miracles he's laid out for you since the beginning of time may never have the opportunity to occur.

If you want God to move on your behalf, you must choose to follow his lead, or the miracles he's laid out for you since the beginning of time may never have the opportunity to occur.

A few summers ago, my obedience opened the door to a miracle that may have saved my parents' lives.

My parents, who are in their seventies, were caught in the Hurricane Rita evacuation. With all of Houston as well as the Beaumont Golden Triangle area on the road, they could only travel three to six miles an hour as the deadly hurricane made a beeline for them.

"Keep your phone on and I'll call you every hour, on the hour," I told my folks. But my mom didn't know how to use her cell phone and ended up accidentally turning the ringer off. Each time I called, the phone answered itself. I could hear their car radio playing weather reports, but no matter how I shouted, neither Mom nor Dad knew I was on the line. This went on for hours. As the night wore on, all I could do was pray. About midnight I finally went to bed.

"Show me what to do," I whispered to the Lord as I drifted into a restless sleep. At 2:00 a.m. my time, my eyes snapped opened. "Lord, should I try to call my parents again?"

"Not yet," a gentle voice whispered to my soul.

I waited till I felt a release. Though only eight minutes had passed since God had first spoken to me, I bolted out of bed and went to the phone and called. It was now 3:08 a.m., Texas time. This time my mom picked up. "Oh, I just saw I had my ringer off. I put it back on and you called," Mom said.

"Mom, where are you?"

"We've only made it to Nacogdoches, Texas. All the shelters that were reserved for Beaumonters are filled with Houstonians, so we'll have to keep moving."

"No!" I said with conviction. "You must get a hotel room."

Mom said, "There's a hotel right across the street from us now."

I knew there was no way this hotel would have a vacancy with over a million people on the road, but I felt led to say, "Try it."

Moments later, my dad returned to the car from the hotel office. He said, "The manager had his no vacancy sign up, but I didn't see it until I rang the bell. He came out and told me he had one room open and we could have it. But I think I'll say no."

"Say yes," I pleaded into the phone. "It's a miracle you found a room. You need to rest."

Dad listened. He and Mom took the room and slept for four hours before continuing their escape to my brother's house in Jackson, Mississippi. Later Mom said, "It was a miracle you called as we came upon that hotel. Your father was so tired he couldn't even find reverse on the car. There was no way he could physically have made it much farther without resting. We wouldn't have stopped if you hadn't called when you did."

It was a miracle. If I had called eight minutes earlier, the phone would not have rung, and even if it had, my parents wouldn't have been near the hotel. God's timing was perfect. What if I hadn't obeyed and waited those eight minutes? What if I had called, gotten no answer, assumed the phone was out of service for the night, and gone back to bed? It hurts even to consider it.

What Might God Call You to Do?

What kinds of things might God ask of you? Here are some instructions God gave his prophets and their people: repent, praise, march or go forth, be confident of his presence, go into battle, stand still, do not be afraid. If you know God has told you to be obedient in any of these areas, do what he's told you to do.

The Fear Factor

If you are not obedient when you know God has spoken to you, what befell the children of Israel upon reaching the Promised Land could happen to you. In Deuteronomy 1:21 we read how God gave the Israelites the hill country of the Amorites. He told them, "Go up and take possession of it. . . . Do not be afraid; do not be discouraged." But instead of going into battle, they sent spies into the land. The spies soon discovered it was a good land full of harvest, but there was a clincher. The men in that locale were as tall as giants. This was terrifying news because it meant their taller opponents had more power and a longer reach with the sword.

Upon hearing this report—never mind God had commanded them to go into battle—they refused, grumbling, "God hates us. The enemy is stronger and taller than us."

Moses told them, "Do not be terrified; do not be afraid of them. The LORD your God, who is going before you, will fight for you, as he did for you in Egypt, before your very eyes, and in the desert. There you saw how the LORD your God carried you, as a father carries his son, all the way you went until you reached this place" (vv. 29–31).

Still they did not trust the Lord. God was not pleased and promised, "Not a man of this evil generation shall see the good land I swore to give your forefathers, except Caleb son of Jephunneh. He will see it, and I will give him and his descendants the land he set his feet on, because he followed the LORD wholeheartedly" (vv. 35–36).

Finally, the people shook off their fear, and said, "Oops, we blew it with the Lord!" Their words and deeds are recorded in Deuteronomy 1:41–46:

> We have sinned against the LORD. We will go up and fight, as the LORD our God commanded us. So every one of you put on his weapons, thinking it easy to go up into the hill country. But the LORD said to me, "Tell them, 'Do not go up and fight, because I will not be with you. You will be defeated by your enemies.'" So I told you, but you would not listen. You rebelled against the LORD's command and in your arrogance you marched up into the hill country. The Amorites who lived in those hills came out against you; they chased you like a swarm of bees and beat you down from Seir all the way to Hormah. You came back and wept before the LORD, but he paid no attention to your weeping and turned a deaf ear to you. And so you stayed in Kadesh many days—all the time you spent there.

Oops, they did it again, and they dearly paid for their disobedience. For two wrongs against God did not set things right; they made things worse. Is obeying God always the best course of action? Yes! 1 Peter 3:16–18 (TLB) says, "Do what is right; then if men speak against you, calling you evil names, they will become ashamed of themselves for falsely accusing you when you have only done what is good. Remember, if God wants you to suffer, it is better to suffer for doing good than for doing wrong!"

> Now, ask yourself this question: "What would I do for God if I weren't afraid?"

In other words, trust God and his direction. There are no guarantees that obeying God will bring you a pain-free life, but it's better to suffer because you trusted God than because you disobeyed him. Yes, we know that God works things together for the good, but we also know what Peter says on the subject in 1 Peter 4:19, "So then, those who suffer according to God's will should commit themselves to their faithful Creator and continue to do good."

Now, ask yourself this question: "What would I do for God if I weren't afraid?"

Spend some quiet time practicing the presence of God with this question in your heart and see where it leads you. God may have been waiting all along for you to ask this question. Seek him and he will give you direction. Pray: "Lord, I give you my fear. Help me to obey you."

Walking with God

When I think back to the most joyful moments in my life, they've usually been the result of God answering my prayers. These times are doubly blessed because I have something to celebrate. I know God was with me and ordained my steps.

I know I'm walking in his ways and in his will. What an exciting place to be.

As I was working on this book, I decided I wasn't going to let anyone interrupt my work. But when ministry, wonderful houseguests, and an avalanche of emails, phone calls, and letters began to consume my time, I started to feel a little panicky. "Help me get it done, Lord," I cried out to him.

I heard his still, small voice speak to my heart. "You will. I'll be with you."

But I wasn't too sure. With more houseguests due to arrive in a few days, it would take a miracle to get this work completed. I continued to fret. I screened emails, phone calls, and told my patient family to treat me as if I was out of town. (They didn't, but they gave my work time a little more consideration than the norm.)

Still, life continued to interrupt me. One morning the phone rang and the caller ID indicated it was the Christian TV show I often host. I love the dear people who work at the station and couldn't resist picking up the phone. It was my friend Trish, the producer. She said, "How would you like to guest host a live show tomorrow?"

I should say no! I told myself. But when I opened my mouth, I said, "I'd love to." Oops! That little detour would take up an entire writing day.

The next morning as I was driving to the station, my thoughts turned to God. "God, I'm sorry," I said. "I don't know why I told Trish yes when I'm under such a deadline. It must be greed. You know how much I love hosting the show; I was just too greedy to say no."

Then I listened and heard the still, sweet voice of the Lord. He whispered to my heart, "You're right where I want you to be."

What a relief. Who needs to worry about deadlines when

you're right where God wants you to be? Who needs to worry about anything, for that matter?

"Oh Lord," I sighed. "I'm so glad to hear that. Being where you want me is so much better than going my own way." With my anxious worries turned off, I couldn't wait to see what God had in store for me in the studio that day.

> Are you where God wants you to be? Have you asked him lately? It's time.

In an earlier chapter, I described that interview with pastor Rene' Whitmore. But the most freeing moment of the entire adventure was knowing I was supposed to be there, that I had permission from the Lord to minister on the air. What freedom and joy.

The live broadcast from the studio was anointed. Then, the next day, I had a record-setting "word count" day, putting me ahead of schedule. My day in Denver had not hurt my writing deadline. Why? It was God. He had me where he wanted me. He equipped me to do the work he'd already prepared for me. Thank you, Lord.

Are you where God wants you to be? Have you asked him lately? It's time.

Pray this:

Dear Lord,

Please help me to be where you want me to be. Guide me, show me, and anoint me for whatever work you have arranged for me. Help me to love my family more deeply, to show more compassion and patience to others, to have boldness in telling others about you. Give me all I need so that my joy may be complete in you. And Lord, today and every day I give you permission to join me, to walk with me, to lead me, to carry my burdens and worries for me. Lord, I commit even my struggles to you. For, Lord, it's your turn.

In Jesus' name,
Amen.

Finding the Miracle

Did you know you have permission to pray for a miracle? But what if, in your prayer for a miracle, you gave God total control of the miracle itself? What if you began to pray prayers like this?

> Lord, I give you my job. Please do a miracle your way and in your will. Lord, now it's your turn.

The final part of this prayer signifies that your fingerprints are off both God's plan as well as the miracle itself. Here's another example:

> Lord, I give you my marriage. Please protect my marriage and give it a glorious miracle your way and in your will. Lord, now it's your turn.

Or how about:

> Lord, I give you my child. Please protect my child but give my child a miracle in your way and in your will. Lord, now it's your turn.

How exciting to take our hands off the controls and let God be God. He's got the wisdom and the power, but does he truly have our permission or even our trust? Are we really willing to say, "Lord, for your kingdom, for your glory and honor, in your will, Lord"? It's time.

Pray this:

> Lord, strengthen my faith and trust in you, by your power and in the name of your Son.

Reread the "miracle-your-turn" prayers above and pray them in as many ways as you can, for as many situations and people as come to mind. Pray this way for yourself as well. It's time you begin to live your life as the miracle it is. It's time you gave God permission to do glorious things in the very situations that once seemed hopeless.

Finished with your assignment? Good. Now we've got only a few more moments to spend together, and here's what I want to tell you: the battle truly belongs to the Lord. As with young David's battle with the giant Goliath, we should not place our trust in earthly weapons but in God. He faced the enemy who mocked his God, and David won the battle with the enemy's own sword.

But in the story of Saul, David did not move to harm the man who was anointed as God's leader of the day, even though Saul had turned on David, vowing to kill him. Still, David said it wasn't his place to kill God's anointed. So follow David's lead and take care that you don't harm God's anointed either.

For example, don't bring down the leadership of your church with your tongue. Don't slander them or use the power of gossip to try to control them or to get your way. However, if someone in the church is harming you or others, confront them directly, in love. If they won't stop, take a witness with you and confront them again according to Matthew 18:15–17:

> How exciting to take our hands off the controls and let God be God. He's got the wisdom and the power, but does he truly have our permission or even our trust? Are we really willing to say, "Lord, for your kingdom, for your glory and honor, in your will, Lord"? It's time.

> If your brother sins against you, go and show him his fault, just between the two of you. If he listens to you, you have won your brother over. But if he will not listen, take one or

two others along, so that "every matter may be established by the testimony of two or three witnesses." If he refuses to listen to them, tell it to the church; and if he refuses to listen even to the church, treat him as you would a pagan or a tax collector.

As you can see, Jesus provided a way to confront the sinner, but you must not try to win this war by repaying evil for evil. That makes you as bad as or perhaps worse than the one you wish to correct.

If your battle is not outside the camp but within the fellowship of those who are called and loved by God, it's not up to you to destroy their life or ministry. That decision belongs to the Lord. You may find yourself dodging a few "arrows" and your feelings may get hurt, but you will survive the attack. Then, when the time is right, you will have the victory God's way and in God's perfect timing.

When you are faced with a battle and you feel God's call to take a stand against the enemy, go into that battle in the name of the Lord. When you're in the battle, let God fight it for you.

So let us rejoice in this: "The victory is not up to us, the victory belongs to God. The battle is his!" (Prov. 21:31).

Praying Scripture

Jesus, as the Father has loved you, you have loved me. Help me to remain in your love. Help me to obey your commands so I will remain in your love, just as you obeyed your Father's commands and remain in his love. (See John 15:9–10.)

Thank you for giving me your Holy Spirit, whom you give to all who obey you. (See Acts 5:32.)

Help me to walk as you did, Jesus, for if I should say, "I know you," but do not do what you command me, then I'm a liar and the truth is not in me. But if I obey your Word, your love is made complete in me. Then they will know you are in me because I walk and act like you. (See 1 John 2:3–6.)

I know you will hear my prayers when I please you through obedience. (See 1 John 3:22.)

If I really love you, I will show it through my obedience and you will help me overcome the world. (See 1 John 5:3.)

In Jesus' name,

Amen.

Conclusion

Discovering Joy

I choose joy. . . . I will invite my God to be the God of circumstance. I will refuse the temptation to be cynical . . . the tool of the lazy thinker. I will refuse to see people as anything less than human beings, created by God. I will refuse to see any problem as anything less than an opportunity to see God.

—Max Lucado

To experience joy, count your blessings and accept your circumstances as gifts to God's glory and opportunities for miracles. Two of the wonderful houseguests I had while I was working on this book were my mom and dad, who flew in from Texas to be with us. One day, after my mom had stopped in to visit Laura in her room, I found her in the kitchen with tears in her eyes.

"What's wrong, Mom?" I asked.

She pulled a tissue from a box. "It's so hard to see my granddaughter so disabled," she said.

"Mom, Laura's not sad. She has a wonderful life. I mean, think about the problems she'll never have. She'll never be strung out on drugs, a runaway, or a teen who's alone and pregnant. She'll never make some horrible choice that will scar her life with heartache and trouble. She's loved, she's happy, she knows God, and she enjoys her life." Mom nodded but didn't speak. I continued, "Did you see how happy she is today?"

"Is she always so happy?"

"Always. Laura has a lot to teach the rest of us about joy, trust, and peace."

My mom had to agree she didn't know anyone with more joy than Laura. And think about it. Here's a girl who is unable to speak but a handful of words who has a worldwide ministry to the depressed. For it's her story that the people from the sea of depression read when they experience GodTest.com. We get letters telling us that Laura's story made people rethink their own circumstances. Laura's story helps people make a decision to live their lives as a living sacrifice to God. That's tremendous, and so were the opportunities God gave Laura and me to speak up before the death of Terri Schiavo, the disabled woman from Florida who was purposely starved to death by means of a court order.

> "Laura has a lot to teach the rest of us about joy, trust, and peace."

I mentioned earlier that Laura is more disabled than Terri was, mainly because Laura is actually on life support, which Terri was not. During Terri's final days, the Denver TV news teams broadcasted live from our driveway, and the miracle of Laura's life made front page news around Colorado.

In fact, one afternoon, with all of Denver stuck in a terrific traffic jam, I was the guest on a popular secular talk show. I spoke to the thousands of drivers stuck along the roadways.

What did I say in all those interviews? I told the reporters and the talk show hosts the truth. "God has a plan and a purpose for everyone, even one as disabled as Laura."

Since I surrendered our situation to God, I've been privileged to live a life of beauty and joy, full of God's loving-kindness. My life, Laura's life, and the lives of my family have been lived in a miracle of God's grace. In fact, Laura was one of the very first readers of this manuscript. As I read it aloud to her, I'd stop at the prayers and say, "Laura, I'm going to let you borrow my voice to pray this prayer to God."

Oh! What joy she had as I prayed to her Lord for her. How holy that time was we spent together with God.

It's ironic that people tend to view our situation as tragic, but God has turned our lives into a miracle. Here's the good news, you can surrender your situation to God and you can live a miracle too.

> "God has a plan and a purpose for everyone, even one as disabled as Laura."

Have you ever wondered why so many homeless victims of hurricanes and tornados tell CNN and Fox, "We are so blessed, we still have each other."

Blessed? Are you kidding me? I'm talking about people who had their houses destroyed, their cars flooded and totaled by falling trees, and they say they're *blessed*? Yes, and they are correct.

Here's another example of blessing. A couple from my church spent Christmas at an orphanage in Mexico. They'd collected used toys to give as Christmas gifts. My son Jimmy, who was about seven at that time, donated a basketful of colorful Happy Meal toys. You know the kind I mean: plastic hopping hamburgers, tiny dolls with green hair, and wind-up cars that spin in circles.

We couldn't wait to hear if the orphans enjoyed the toys. They did. When each child had selected a toy from the basket, there were toys left over. The orphans decided to share out of their abundance and delivered the rest of the toys to the local street children that Christmas Day.

Out of their abundance? Their generosity made me see abundance in a whole new light. These children are wealthier than I ever imagined.

Do you recognize the abundance God has given you? Ask him to show you, then respond with the best kind of prayer: praise!

Praise God

The secret of David's success was not only his trust in the Lord but also his thankful heart. Many of his praise songs are recorded in the book of Psalms, including this one in Psalm 63. As you read it, praise God yourself through the words.

> O God, you are my God,
>   earnestly I seek you;
> my soul thirsts for you,
>   my body longs for you,
> in a dry and weary land
>   where there is no water.
> I have seen you in the sanctuary
>   and beheld your power and your glory.
> Because your love is better than life,
>   my lips will glorify you.
> I will praise you as long as I live,
>   and in your name I will lift up my hands.
> My soul will be satisfied as with the richest of foods;
>   with singing lips my mouth will praise you.
> On my bed I remember you;
>   I think of you through the watches of the night.
> Because you are my help,

I sing in the shadow of your wings.
My soul clings to you;
    your right hand upholds me.

verses 1–8

Take a moment to thank God for all the blessings he has given you. Remember to live your life as a prayer, practicing the presence of God. Rick Warren said, "Everything you do can be spending time with God if he is invited to be a part of it and you stay aware of his presence."[1]

Praying Scripture

Lord, you are near me when my heart is broken and when I call upon you in truth. You fulfill the desires of my heart because I fear you. You hear me and save me. (See Ps. 145:18–19.)

I call on you, Lord, when I'm distressed, and you answer me. (See Ps. 120:1.)

I have confidence to approach you and know that if I ask anything, according to your will, you hear me. Because you hear the prayers I've prayed that are in your will, I have what I've asked for. (See 1 John 5:14–15.)

Because I belong to you, you hear me when I cry out to you. You deliver me from my troubles. (See Ps. 34:17.)

I call to you, God, and you save me. No matter the time, you always hear my voice. (See Ps. 55:16–17.)

Therefore, I will be joyful always. I will pray continually. I will give thanks in all circumstances, for this is your will for me through your Son, Christ Jesus. (See 1 Thess. 5:16–18.)

For this reason I kneel before you, Father, the Creator of heaven and earth. I pray out of your glorious riches to be strengthened with power through your Spirit in my inner being, so that Christ may dwell in my heart through faith. And I pray to be rooted and established in love, so I will have the power, together with all the saints, to grasp how wide and long and high and deep is the love of Christ, and to know this love that surpasses knowledge—so I may be filled with the measure of all the fullness of God. (See Eph. 3:14–19.)

In Jesus' name,

Amen.

Final Words

Thank you for allowing me to speak into your life through these pages as we've laughed together, cried together, and prayed together. I hope that God has done a work in your prayer life, and I pray that his work will continue. In the meantime, keep on praying and do what you know you ought to do.

Not long ago, I got an email from a man who said, "I really needed a good sermon so I got my video camera out, pointed it at myself, and preached my heart out. Then I watched the tape. I have to tell you, it was the best sermon I ever heard. It really helped me."

It's true, we know what we ought to do, so let's pledge to do it: serve the Lord, forgive wrongs, give our burdens to him, thank him for the blessings, and let him fight our battles.

Let's end our time together with this prayer:

Dear Lord,

Thank you so much for this opportunity to draw closer to you. Remind me to stay close and that it's you who will go before me, carry my burdens, and fight my battles.

Lord, together we pray that you would heal our hearts, our families, our land, and turn hearts back to you. We humbly ask you to forgive us and our land for crimes and sins against you. Lord, we pray for a miracle. Use us to see this come to pass.

Thank you, Father. It's your turn.

In Jesus' name,

Amen.

Notes

Introduction

    1. William Temple, www.BrainyQuote.com.

Chapter 1: Project Prayer

    1. Letter from "Why Not Be Dead," www.GodTest.com.

Chapter 2: The Five Keys to Power Prayer

    1. Aldous Huxley, www.onlyinternet.net.
    2. Rick Warren, *The Purpose Driven Life* (Grand Rapids: Zondervan, 2002), 87.

Chapter 4: What to Pray to Help You Realize God's Presence

    1. Letter from "Lonely for God," www.GodTest.com.

Chapter 5: What to Pray When Your Burdens Are Heavy

    1. Andrew Murray, http://www.praybig.com/media/Quotes.html.
    2. Letter from visitor, www.GodTest.com.
    3. Linda Evans Shepherd, *Encouraging Hands, Encouraging Hearts* (Ann Arbor: Servant Publications, 1999), 164.
    4. Warren, 85.

Chapter 6: What to Pray When You've Been Betrayed

    1. *Da Jesus Book* (Wycliffe Bible Translations, 2000), 132.
    2. Leonard Ravenhill, www.psalm121.ca/.

Chapter 7: What to Pray When Everything Goes Wrong

1. Charles Haddon Spurgeon, www.epm.org.

Chapter 8: What to Pray in Difficult Financial Situations

1. Karen O'Connor, adapted by Karen from "It's Not About Money After All," *The Lookout,* August 8, 1999.

2. Marva J. Dawn, *Keeping the Sabbath Wholly* (Grand Rapids: Wm. B. Eerdmans, 1989), 28.

Chapter 9: Praying for Others

1. Eva Marie Everson, adapted from "911 Focus," in *Intimate Encounters with God* (Colorado Springs: Honor Books, 2003), 8–9.

Chapter 11: Why God Answers

1. John Bunyan, www.psalm121.ca/.

Conclusion

1. Warren, 89.

Reader's Guide

When You Don't Know What to Pray

Study Guide for Personal Reflection and Discussion

The world is more chaotic than ever with more war, natural disasters, debt, and heartache. How could there be a loving God when so many things have gone wrong? Where was God when we asked him to bless us? Was he listening? Could it be we're not praying with the right words or attitude?

I can't judge your heart, but I do know God's great loving-kindness and mercy. Whether you believe your prayers have been answered or not, I believe God is calling out to you in his loving way. He's calling you to awaken; church to arise from your slumber.

The way you've understood prayer in the past needs to be challenged, expanded, and explored. Prayer may not be all you thought it was, because, in fact, it may be more. It's time to pray in a way that will change your perspective about God and his plan for your life. Despite the hardships you may have endured, God is even now turning your life into a miracle. When you learn how to pray in God's will, you will watch that miracle unfold.

You are loved and not forgotten. God has good purposes for those who love him who are called to walk in his ways. Let's wake up to be one of his children of purpose who will make a difference in our world and in his kingdom to come. Get ready to pray through this book. If you are not in a discussion group, jot your answers into a journal or notepad. Let us wake up to joy and a thankful heart. But first, let us pray . . .

1: Project Prayer

1. Linda tells a story about a woman named Barb who was angry at both God and herself. How did Barb's anger interfere with her relationship with God? How did Barb get set free?
2. How can one have guaranteed prayer results? Why was Simon unsuccessful in securing the anointing of God to heal others? What danger did he evoke by trying to buy the power of God?
3. What was the powerful prayer that Linda prayed that changed her life? Do you need to pray a prayer like that? Write your own prayer to give your situation to God.
4. Why is friendship with God difficult when we feel angry at God, ourselves, or others? Why does it hurt us to hold a secret or not-so-secret grudge against God? What four results would you receive if you were able to "let go" of any grudges and reconcile with God?
5. What was the flaw in Why Not's death wish? Does Jesus weep with those who grieve? How do we know? What does God want us to do with our burdens and circumstances? Why?

6. What does 1 Peter 5:7 mean when it says to "cast all your anxieties on him"? Can we really trust God with our burdens? How?

7. How would you write a prayer to cast your burdens and cares on God?

2: The Five Keys to Power Prayer

1. Jesus was the first to pray such a power prayer. Based on his prayer, known as the Lord's Prayer, name five keys to power prayer and give an example of how to use each key to create a prayer of your own.

2. What does it mean to repent? Why does God advise us to repent? Linda talks about two major benefits a person will receive when they repent of their sin. What are they? Can you think of an example to share about a time you received one of these benefits?

3. How does Linda's escape from the nest of baby rattlesnakes apply to a way we can get out of sin? Read 1 Corinthians 6:9–11 and give examples of how a person can step away from different kinds of sin. Why is it important to ask God for the power to repent?

4. Why does God answer our prayers? Why did God answer the prayer Linda prayed for Kate?

5. Is it okay to ask God for specific prayer requests? Give examples of times God answered specific prayers.

6. Why does God say no to some prayer requests, like the request the apostle Paul prayed to "remove the thorn in his flesh"? Why didn't Paul continue to fight with God after it was clear God's answer was no? What can we learn from Paul's attitude?

7. Does God always hear our prayer requests? Jesus thanked God for hearing his prayer request when he

prayed that Lazarus would be raised from the dead. What can we learn from this?

8. Take turns praying for specific prayer requests for either yourself or the people in the group (or people you know).

3: *What to Pray for Yourself*

1. Why do you think it's so hard to really believe in and feel God's love for us? What would it take to help you to understand it? Take a moment to pray for a deeper understanding of God's love for yourself and everyone in your group.

2. According to Linda, what is the "divine question" and how did Jesus answer it?

3. Seeing Jesus die on the cross was part of Lucifer's demonic plan. How and why did his plan backfire?

4. Discuss how Louisa May Alcott's character Edith, from *The Inheritance*, parallels who we are in Christ.

5. Read the "Knowing Who You Are in Christ" list of attributes aloud. Pick one of the attributes to your identity in Christ and explain why it's meaningful to you.

6. Read John 17:1–26. List the things Christ prayed for us in his closing benediction before he suffered the cross.

4: *What to Pray to Help You Realize God's Presence*

1. What are some reasons we may not be able to feel God's presence? Which of these reasons can we do something about?

2. Not only do we need to invite God into all areas of our lives, we need to entertain his presence. List several ways to do that.

3. Why did Sheila feel God was for everyone but her? Compose a prayer that someone like Sheila could pray to help her understand that God is for her.

4. How does having a broken heart keep us from feeling God's presence? How did Kathy begin to feel God's presence when her mom was in the hospital? What are the two things Linda suggests you do if you have a broken heart?

5. Read Psalm 34 and list all the ways God delivers those who cry out to him.

6. How does the story of the princess relate to God's great love for us?

5: What to Pray When Your Burdens Are Heavy

1. What is the divine benefit of trouble? How and why does it point us to God?

2. If you were to write a letter to help the suicidal GodTest.com visitor, what would you say?

3. Read Psalm 68:19. Review your list of all the cares you would like to cast on God. If you haven't already done so, name your cares in a prayer, giving each to God.

4. Read Luke 11:46. Why was Jesus angry at the religious leaders of the day? Why was this opposite of what is written in 1 Peter 5:7?

5. Read the poem "It's Your Turn" aloud again as a prayer.

6. How did God heal Linda's heart when she realized he was not going to further heal Laura's disabilities?

7. How will you put on the full armor of God? What difference will it make to your life?

6: *What to Pray When You've Been Betrayed*

1. In *Da Jesus Book*, we are warned not to stay in a "huhu" with others so God will not stay in a "huhu" with us. Based on Mark 11:25, translate the word *huhu* and think of those people you have a current huhu against. Pray and ask God to help you let go of those huhus so God will let go of his huhus against you.

2. List the benefits that Betrayed would gain if she could forgive those who wronged her. How would it be possible for Betrayed to forgive such terrible wrongs? If you were trying to give Betrayed wise counsel, what would you tell her?

3. Was it okay for Linda to be bitter against Sharon Cain's killer? Can Sharon's murder be justified? What did Linda learn about forgiveness in that situation? Which of these truths can you apply to your life?

4. Can God forgive murderers like the man from Beaumont who killed the two ladies in a bank robbery? Why? How? Think of the worst thing you've ever done. Read Colossians 1:13–14 and then answer this question: Can God really forgive me for what I did? Has he already? If you're not sure, take time to apologize to God now, through his Son, Jesus, then spend some time knowing you are forgiven.

5. Why did Abigail need to apologize for her husband? How did that apology save her life? Can you think of peaceful words you need to deliver to or on behalf of another?

6. Why do we need to apologize to others when we find ourselves in conflict? Is there anyone to whom you owe an apology? Ask God to give you an opportunity to apologize, and then act on it. If it means making a phone call or writing a letter or email today, do it.

7: What to Pray When Everything Goes Wrong

1. Think about Linda's very bad day. List all the things that went wrong with the day, and then list all the things that went right. Do you see how counting blessings helps give you a new perspective? Now, think about your day. Of course you had things go wrong, but try to change your perspective by focusing on what went right. Make a list.

2. Read a part of God's response to Job's "why" question in Job 40:1–14. What is God's point? How does Job respond? What does this exchange between God and Job mean?

3. Think of the story Linda shared about the New York fireman who died of cancer. How did what happened on 9/11 change the fireman's sister's perspective of the tragedy? Do you think God may have a different perspective on what we consider our tragedies? Can you give examples?

4. What is the difference between mercy and grace?

5. Is it a good idea to give God our very lives daily? Do you think we can trust God that much or do you think God would use our submission to him to play dirty tricks on us? Why or why not? How much control do we really have over our lives?

6. According to Linda, what are the three things we should pray when we are going through a difficult time? Turn those three things into a prayer.

8: What to Pray in Difficult Financial Situations

1. Read Matthew 6:19–21. What's the difference between earthly treasures and heavenly treasure? Which is best to collect? Which treasures do you wish to add to your collection?

2. It was reported that a multimillion-dollar lottery winner committed suicide. Apparently, even with all his millions, he was unable to buy happiness. Do you think it is possible to buy happiness? Do you think some people would have happier lives without wealth? Is it wrong to be wealthy?

3. Read Philippians 4:19. Make a list of needs you would like to offer to the Lord, through Jesus. Stop and ask God to meet these needs.

4. How did Karen O'Connor recover from financial debt? What was one thing that impressed you about her story? Name Karen's four financial disciplines. Explain which of these disciplines you want to strive to achieve and why.

5. Read Matthew 14:13–20. How is this story like the story Linda told about her ministry's budget goals? Do you think God could multiply what you have to meet your needs? Ask him in prayer.

6. Can we run up our credit cards frivolously then ask God to pay our bills? Under what conditions can we seek God when we need help with a bill? Is there a bill you need to dedicate to God? Pray and do so, then determine how God may be calling you to take financial responsibility.

7. Do you think 10 percent is enough to give as a tithe? Pray and seek the Lord to see if this is the amount he wants you to give. Sit quietly before him on this issue. He may or may not choose to answer immediately, but make yourself ready to apply his answer when he gives it.

9: Praying for Others

1. Read Galatians 6:2. Why do you think we are to carry each other's burdens? How does one do that? What

burden do you have for another? Stop and take it to the Lord in prayer, right now.

2. What would have happened if Moses had not prayed for the children of Israel when they built a golden calf to worship? If you knew that your prayers could make such a significant difference when prayed on the behalf of others, how would that change your prayer life?

3. Read Luke 5:17–26. Jesus had the power to heal the sick and forgive sins. Which of these two gifts is most important, to be healed or to be forgiven? Why did the Pharisees think Jesus' words about forgiving sins were blasphemous? Were the words of Jesus an insult to God? Why or why not?

4. Reread Luke 6:28–29 and decide exactly for whom God is calling us to pray. Are there people in your life you need to add to your prayer list? Stop and pray for them now.

5. Read Hebrews 7:23–25. Does Jesus pray for us? Why? What do you think he accomplishes in his prayers? What kinds of things do you think he prays for you?

6. Why is it important to forgive others? Why did forgiveness make a difference in Marie's prayers for her family? Do you have people for whom you pray who need your forgiveness? Stop and ask God to help give you the power to forgive and ask him to forgive each of these persons with his power, through you.

7. If you are in a group setting, ask each person in the group what they would like for you to agree with them in prayer, regarding a specific prayer request, then pray a prayer of agreement with them as a group. If you can't agree with a particular request, find a way to come to an agreement with their request, perhaps on a different level. Once you agree, pray the prayer of agreement in

the name of Jesus. If you are not in a group setting, seek out a friend to pray in a prayer of agreement.

10: *Can We Really Trust God with Our Prayers?*

1. Read Romans 8:28. Explain why you should trust God with your circumstances.
2. How was Joseph able to stay cheerful despite his circumstances? How can you?
3. Read Genesis 50:19–20. Why did Joseph forgive his wayward brothers?
4. Do you think when God is with us we couldn't be safer? Why or why not? Read Daniel 3:16–18. What did Shadrach, Meshach, and Abednego say of the danger they faced? Who was in the flames with them?
5. What should you do when you are overcome with fear? Do you have the right to pray that the enemy be bound? In whose name should you pray?
6. When God leads us to take the next step, what should we do? If you have a question about what that next step should be regarding a circumstance you are in, stop and ask God to show you. Remember, God may not answer immediately, but his answers are never too late.

11: *Why God Answers*

1. Think of a prayer that God has answered, either in your own life or from a story in the Bible. Go over the top ten reasons why God answers prayer found in the beginning of this chapter and try to identify why you think God answered the request you are thinking of.
2. Could it be that God is a jealous God because he's jealous for our time and attention? Perhaps God wants us to turn from false gods in order to protect us. Make a

list of the false gods we worship in our society today, and then lay each of these gods down before God. For example, pray: "I surrender the god of (money) to you, Lord. You supply my needs. I do not need to worship money."

3. Is it possible to pray to the Lord through our tears? Why? How? Are there other ways one can pray to God?

4. How did Elijah hear God's voice on the mountain? What are the ways God speaks to us today? If you can, share an example with your group or write an example in a journal.

5. Read 1 John 4:1–3. Why does Linda ask, "Lord, is that really you?" when she thinks God is speaking to her. What counterfeit voices are in the world?

6. Discuss the kinds of things the enemy will whisper to our spirits. Ask God, in the name of Jesus, to silence this voice now. Pray this prayer again whenever you think it's warranted.

12: Our Response

1. What are the kinds of things that could happen if you refuse to do what you clearly know God wants you to do?

2. Review the Ten Commandments in Exodus 20:1–17. Based on those Scriptures, make a list of ways we can obey God.

3. Think about, write down, or share about a time you had to make a hard choice and do the right thing. Do you think it had a positive impact on (a) you, (b) someone else, or (c) your relationship with God? Why or why not?

4. How does one double-check if they have heard from the Lord? If one does hear from the Lord, why be obedient to the call? Reread the list of the things God asks of his prophets. Which of these is God saying to you?

5. Write a list of things you would do if you weren't afraid. Dedicate this list to God. Ask him to take away your fear and direct your path according to his will regarding your list.

6. According to the story recorded in the first chapter of Deuteronomy, how did the children of Israel do wrong in the eyes of God? What did they do to correct it? Why was their follow-up action incorrect? How should they have responded?

7. In accordance with the story of David and Saul, what should you do if you are in conflict with someone in ministry leadership?

Conclusion: Discovering Joy

1. Think of the orphans in Mexico who gave out of their abundance. List ways you can share your abundance with others.

2. Create a short sermon (one to two minutes) that you need to hear and preach it to yourself or your group, or jot it down.

3. What was your favorite lesson in the book and why?

4. What was your favorite story from the book and why?

5. What was your favorite prayer from the book and why?

6. Pray the last prayer in the book again.

Linda Evans Shepherd is a beloved author, a radio and TV personality, the president of Right to the Heart Ministries, co-president of Web TV 4 Women and Could Be TV, an international speaker, the founder and leader of Advanced Writers and Speakers Association, and the publisher of Right to the Heart of Women ezine, which goes to women leaders of the church. She's been married thirty years to Paul and has two children, Laura and Jimmy.

Linda has written more than thirty books including co-authoring the Potluck Club series and the Potluck Catering Club series, and *Share Jesus Without Fear*, written with Bill Fay and now in over fifty languages.

For more information about Linda, see VisitLinda.com. For more information about *When You Don't Know What to Pray* or other books in this series, see WhatToPray.org.